CYPRUS

with Local Tips

*The author's special recommendations are
highlighted in yellow throughout this guide*

There are five symbols to help you find your way around this guide:

Marco Polo's top recommendations – the best in each category

sites with a scenic view

places where the local people meet

places where young people get together

(100/A1)
pages and coordinates for the Road Atlas
(U/A1) *coordinates for the City Map of Nicosia inside back cover*
(O) *area not covered by maps*

MARCO ⊕ POLO

Travel guides and language guides in this series:

Algarve • Amsterdam • Australia • Berlin • Brittany • California
Channel Islands • Costa Brava/Barcelona • Costa del Sol/Granada
Côte d'Azur • Crete • Cuba • Cyprus • Eastern USA • Florence • Florida
Gran Canaria • Greek Islands/Aegean • Ibiza • Ireland • Istanbul • Lanzarote
London • Mallorca • Malta • New York • New Zealand • Normandy • Paris
Prague • Rhodes • Rome • Scotland • South Africa • Southwestern USA
Tenerife • Turkish Coast • Tuscany • Venice • Western Canada

French • German • Italian • Spanish

*Marco Polo would be very interested to hear your
comments and suggestions. Please write to:*

North America:
Marco Polo North America
70 Bloor Street East
Oshawa, Ontario, Canada
(B) 905-436-2525

United Kingdom:
GeoCenter International Ltd
The Viables Centre
Harrow Way
Basingstoke, Hants RG22 4BJ

*Cover photograph: Rocks of Aphrodite, Petra tou Romiou (Mauritius: World P.: Holt)
Photos: Author (4); Lade: Ege (44); Mauritius: Bergmann (84, 87), Bohnacker (39),
Gierth (12, 62, 74, 78), Hubatka (99), Nägele (24, 52, 61), Photo Bank (45), Pigneter (30),
Waldkirch (26, 29); Schapowalow: Picker (11), Torino (17, 40, 48, 72); Transglobe: Svensson (8);
Touristik-Marketing GmbH (20, 23)*

3rd revised edition 2000
© Mairs Geographischer Verlag, Ostfildern, Germany
Author: Alfred Janssen
Translator: Joan Clough
English edition 2000: Gaia Text
Editorial director: Ferdinand Ranft
Chief editor: Marion Zorn
Cartography for the Road Atlas: © Mairs Geographischer Verlag
Design and layout: Thienhaus/Wippermann
Printed in Germany

CONTENTS

Discover Cyprus!

Scenic beauty, superb beaches, historic places and culinary delights lure visitors to this lovely island

In the far eastern corner of the Mediterranean lies an enchanted isle. Third largest in the Mediterranean and the birthplace of Aphrodite, goddess of love, Cyprus is called Kípros in Greek.

It has long held an honoured place in the catalogues of reputable travel agencies and is enormously popular amongst English-speaking holidaymakers. Only about 4½ hours by air from London, it is blessed with a mild climate, which ensures sunny holidays all year round.

Nevertheless, Cyprus has not yet been overrun with mass tourism. Perhaps its natural beauty and magnificent beaches, its historic places and the culinary delights it offers are simply not as well known as the island deserves. More significantly, unsettled political conflicts in the region and on the island itself may have deterred many potential holidaymakers. As is well

A favourite photo motif: the handsome Hala Sultan Tekké Mosque in Lárnaka

known, the northern part of Cyprus was invaded by Turkey in 1974 and is occupied by about 40,000 Turkish soldiers. UN Blue Berets have been stationed on Cyprus since 1964. A glance at the atlas shows that the Syrian coast is only about 100 km distant and Egypt 350 km away – Near Eastern flashpoints feel too close for comfort.

Don't worry. You can enjoy holidays on Cyprus just as peacefully and carefree as you might anywhere else in the Mediterranean. Far from Europe's industrial centres and polluted rivers, you'll bask on pristine beaches and swim in limpid azure waters. The famously hospitable and cosmopolitan Cypriots will see to it that your stay is delightful in every respect. Surprises will await you every day you spend on this beautiful island.

The Cyprus coastline is so variegated that, no matter what their preferences, beach aficionados are sure to find much more than they have bargained for. Endlessly long sandy beaches fringe the east coast

History at a glance

7000–1050 BC
Cyprus is inhabited by tribes from Asia Minor

294 B–AD 391
Cyprus first becomes a Ptolemaic province and then a Roman one in 58 BC, with Páfos as its capital. In AD 45 the Apostle Paul visits the island as a missionary

391–1191
Cyprus is part of the East Roman Empire and later of the Byzantine Empire, but from 647 to AD 965 also pays tribute to invading Arabs

1191–1489
Cyprus is ruled by a dynasty of Frankish kings, the Lusignans, who take part in the Crusades

1489–1571
Venice takes possession of and rules the island

1571–1878
Cyprus becomes part of the Ottoman Empire; many Turks settle on the island in this period

1878–1925
Under the Cyprus Convention Great Britain stations troops on Cyprus, which is strategically situated near the Suez Canal

1925–60
Cyprus becomes a British Crown colony in 1925; from 1931 the call for union (Énosis) with Greece grows louder. In 1950 the newly appointed Archbishop of Cyprus, Makários III, is designated spokesman for union with Greece. From 1955 to 1958 Greek Cypriots fight in the EOKA resistance organization for union with Greece

1960–74
Cyprus becomes a sovereign state at last. Archbishop Makários III is elected its first president. By 1963 fierce fighting breaks out between Greek and Turkish Cypriots, leading ultimately to civil war. The first UN peace force is dispatched to Cyprus in 1964. From then on EOKA combat units, their members still desperately hoping for union with Greece, continue to launch numerous attacks on Turkish Cypriots

From 1974
Cyprus illegally partitioned. On 15 July 1974 Makários is deposed in a putsch sparked off by the military junta that usurped power in Greece in 1967. He does not return to Cyprus until December 1974. Turkish forces have already conquered over a third of the island between 20 July and 16 August. Makários III dies in 1977. In 1983 a Turkish Cypriot, Rauf Denktash, proclaims the 'Turkish Republic of Northern Cyprus' in the occupied part of the island. To this day it has been officially recognized only by Turkey. The present president of the Republic of Cyprus, Gláfcos Clerídes, is elected to office in 1993

north of Famagústa as well as the south coast at Lárnaka. Many lovely sandy coves dot the coast near Agía Nápa, west of Páfos, and in the occupied north near Keryneia. At Pólis there are pebble beaches. Off the Ágíos Geórgios Alemánnos Monastery you can enter the water from rocks that have been conveniently polished over the millennia by wind and waves. And then there are some grand rocky coasts. Perhaps the most impressive are in the south between Koúrion and the Rocks of Aphrodite.

The coastal plains are cultivated intensively. Vineyards alternate with small fields of grain and olive and carob groves. Citrus fruits of all kinds are grown near Límassol and Páfos. Potatoes are the leading crop at Agía Nápa. Páfos is surrounded by banana plantations and peanut fields. Two salt lakes near the coast provide an exotic touch. When flooded during the winter months, they are a magnet for clouds of flamingoes. In summer they are salt pans.

Three of the island's five large cities are strung out along the south coast: Límassol (pop. 147,000), Lárnaka (pop. 6,500) and Páfos (pop. 35,000). Dominated by contemporary architecture, much of it high-rise buildings, all three cities are modern and elegant. The strikingly cosmopolitan ambience of these cities is not surprising when one remembers that all three mushroomed from dusty, small towns into major international commercial and banking centres, ports and holiday venues only after the 1974 Turkish invasion.

Being new, hotels in these cities boast a high standard of comfort. The concrete eyesores marring some Spanish and Italian holiday centres or occupied Famagústa, where all hotels were built before the 1974 invasion, are not encountered here. Built on a human scale, hotels in the south blend into the landscape. Their personnel is polite and well trained and the management is invariably professional.

Restaurants, shops, banks and all businesses employ personnel who speak English to a high standard. Menus, signs and road signs are in two langauges (Greek-English transcription) throughout the southern part of the Republic of Cyprus, although not in the occupied north.

Excellent spoken and written English and a good commercial infrastructure are probably a legacy of long years of British rule. After 1878 British troops were stationed on the island and from 1925 to 1960 London ruled Cyprus as a British crown colony. Although the Republic of Cyprus does not yet have a university, many young people still study in Great Britain or the US. The older generation lived under and worked for the British in Cyprus or in Britain. Great Britain still has two large military installations between Límassol and Páfos and between Lárnaka and Agía Nápa, where Cypriots are employed. The 20,000 British nationals living on these bases are important for the island economy.

Cyprus has repeatedly been subjected to foreign domination in the course of its long history. As early as 9,000 years ago, predating the Neolithic Stonehenge I complex, Irish chamber tombs and Maltese megalithic temples, well organized settlements with round houses on stone footings, had already been built on Cyprus. You can view the impressive ruins of an early Neolithic settlement at Choirokoitía (pronounced Khirokitía).

History buffs will certainly find enough to keep them busy on Cyprus. Even on the beaches: as Greek mythology has it, Aphrodite first trod terra firma on the pebbles of the beach off the Cliffs of Aphrodite, called by Greek-speaking Cypriots 'É Pétra tou Romióu'. She was born of the foam enveloping the genitals of Uranus, which his son Cronos had cast into the sea. On Mt Olympus, home of the gods in northern Greece, she was goddess of love and of all things erotic. She is still commemorated in the Baths of Aphrodite, where, legend has it, she indulged in secret dalliance with her lover Akamas near Pólis on Cyprus.

A goddess of fertility was worshipped on Cyprus before the Achaean Greeks reached the island towards the close of the 2nd millennium BC. From the 1st millennium BC she was venerated as Aphrodite in the old sanctuary near Páfos consecrated to the goddess of fertility. The Páfos Aphrodite sanctuary

A detail of one of the many mosaics at Páfos

8

attracted votaries from all over the ancient world. By this time Cyprus had been called the 'island of Aphrodite', an epithet that is still much highlighted in contemporary tourism advertising.

Not far from Aphrodite's Páfos precincts, a beautiful young god was venerated in Koúrion: Apollo. However, in his sanctuary, most of the extant buildings date from the Roman era. Festival performances of plays and concerts are still staged for visitors and locals in the meticulously restored Roman amphitheatre in the ancient city of Koúrion.

All sorts of performances are also held in the Roman Odeon at Páfos, a city particularly rich in ancient monuments. In fact, Páfos is, to put it in modern terms, a giant archaeological theme park, where you can see Roman mosaics in a remarkably good state of preservation and eerie Ptolemaic graves juxtaposed with the flagellation column, where the Apostle Paul was once publicly scourged.

St Paul brought Christianity to Cyprus. Another Apostle, St Barnabas, became the island's first bishop. Numerous ruined basilicas on a grand scale as well as a mosaic ranking amongst the marvellous mosaics of Ravenna attest to the considerable size of the Early Christian communities on Cyprus in the early centuries of the East Roman or Byzantine Empire from about AD 400 to the Arab incursions after 647.

Some churches in Cypriot villages and towns like Geroskípou and Lárnaka are over 1,000 years old. Lárnaka's earliest church is consecrated to St Lazarus, whom Christ raised from the dead (John XI.1 – 44). After his resurrection, Lazarus is said to have become Lárnaka's first bishop. After his second death, he was buried here. The venerable church of Agía Paraskeví in Geroskípou is consecrated to a martyred saint in the Orthodox canon whose eyes were gouged out by pagan officials. The Orthodox Church venerates Agía Paraskeví as the patron saint of sufferers from eye disease. Her icon is invariably smothered by little plaques on which a pair of eyes is represented, votive offerings from devout Orthodox Christians whose eye disease has been alleviated or healed through the saint's intercession.

Greek Cypriots are still deeply religious Orthodox Christians. The Orthodox Church has been the main unifying force that has preserved Cypriot identity over 800 years of foreign domination (since 1191). No wonder, then, that the influence of the Church is still pervasive in both public and private life on the island. Registry-office marriages and divorce were not legalized in the Republic of Cyprus until 1990, but are still rare. The Church and some monasteries are great landowners, have shares in vineyards and a brewery and own hotels and other businesses. After the death of Makários III, who was both Archbishop and President of the Cypriot Republic from 1960 to 1977, the Church continued to exert a strong influence on Cypriot domestic politics. Even Cypriots who are members of the Cypriot communist party

(AKEL), which still receives about a quarter of all votes cast at elections, only rarely fail to attend divine service on religious holidays.

Visitors to Cyprus will undoubtedly find the churches in the Tróodos Mountains fascinating. Looking like granaries with their oddly pitched roofs almost sweeping the ground, they represent an architectural style unique to the region. Superb medieval frescoes have been preserved in over 20 of these churches. For this reason they have all been designated UNESCO World Cultural Heritage site monuments despite their modest exteriors. You should at least try to visit the little church at Asínou, if you want to feel that you really do know something about Cyprus.

The Tróodos is one of two mountain ranges on the island. The other is the Pendedáktylos Range, also known as the Kyrénia Mountains. Rising to an elevation of 1,026 m, the Pendedáktylos Mountains stretch over 100 km across the northern coast of Cyprus. The Tróodos covers over 60 square km. Rising to an elevation of 1,951 m, it takes up the western part of the island and much of the south. Between the two mountain ranges a broad plain (elevation 100 m) straddles the island from Mórfou in the west to Famagústa in the east. Nicosía (Greek: Lefkosía), the capital of the Republic of Cyprus, is in this plain.

The Tróodos Massif consists of a maze of low mountain chains. Cherries and walnuts, apples and pears, plums and many other varieties of fruits and nuts thrive in its river valleys. Wine is grown to an elevation of over 1,000 m. Other regions of the Tróodos are thickly wooded, notably in the west. Small mountain streams never run dry, not even in summer. Near Páno Plátres there is a waterfall. Numerous reservoirs of all sizes catch the winter rain and quite a few village communities raise trout in large ponds.

The entire Tróodos region is criss-crossed by a network of good roads. Attractive, well-marked nature paths cater to backpackers and hikers. Picturesquely rickety old buses clatter to all villages. Some of the mountain villages, notably Páno Plátres and Kakopetriá, are entirely given over to the tourist trade. Others, however, are untouched by the ravages of time and tourism. In such villages weddings are still celebrated in the traditional way by the entire community, and any tourists who happen to be there will be invited. Every Sunday morning baptisms in Tróodos monasteries are followed by huge communal feasts.

The poverty that may once have seemed idyllic to Central European tourists in particular has been overcome. The Republic of Cyprus is a prosperous country. Even in the remotest rural regions, comfortable houses with all modern conveniences have replaced hovels. Farmers no longer ride donkeys and mules; they drive cars and tractors.

When driving through mountain valleys, you'll pass through quite a few nearly de-

Olive groves adorn the coasts of Cyprus

about 100,000. Their ancestors came to the island during the over 300 years of Ottoman rule between 1571 and 1878. Since 1974 more than 50,000 mainland Turks have settled in the occupied north in violation of international law. They were all immediately granted the right to vote in elections held in north Cyprus.

When the Venetians ruled Cyprus, they tried to secure it against Ottoman invasion with a chain of forts across the island. Three of them still stand in the Kyrénia Mountains.

The Crusaders and, after them, the Venetians also surrounded the important cities of Nicosía, Famagústa and Keryneia with fortification walls. The original walls still encircle the old towns of Nicosía and Famagústa. The old towns and markets of these cities have retained the rather Oriental flavour that was still characteristic of Cyprus in the 1930s. The economic upturn the southern part of the island has undergone over the past few decades has changed most cities on Cyprus beyond recognition.

All Cypriot cities are rewarding to visit, both for their atmosphere and shopping as well as for their superb museums, historic monuments and archaeological sites. Ethnographic museums figure as prominently as archaeological ones; other museums are devoted to Byzantine art and modern history. In travelling around this beautiful island, third largest in the Mediterranean after Sicily and Sardinia, you'll survey its turbulent history and sophisticated culture.

serted or even entirely abandoned villages. Turkish Cypriots lived in them until 1974. After the July 1974 invasion by Turkish troops, they left for the north. The 1974 war, which lasted a month, was sparked off by the then military dictators of Greece, who backed an abortive putsch against Cypriot President Makários III with the purpose of annexing Cyprus. To prevent annexation by Greece, the Turkish government felt justified in intervening in Cyprus. In violation of international law, Turkish troops still occupy territory in the north comprising nearly 40 per cent of the island's surface area. The 1974 invasion gave rise to mass migrations. Over 150,000 Greek Cypriots fled south from the Turkish-occupied north. At the same time, more than 45,000 Turkish Cypriots moved north. The island population totals 730,000, of whom a quarter are refugees. Now about 630,000 Greek Cypriots live in the south. The Turkish Cypriot population of the occupied north stands at

From Byzantium to temples

History has left its mark, not merely in stone, but also on the political issues confronting Cyprus today

Foreigners

For the past 800 years foreigners have held the fate of Cyprus in their hands. From 1191 the island's rulers spoke a different language, practised a different form of Christianity or even adhered to a different religion altogether. The first to arrive were the Roman Catholic Crusaders, then the Venetians, followed by the Turks and ultimately the British. Without consulting the Cypriots, Great Britain, Greece and Turkey gave the island people the constitution according to which today's Republic of Cyprus is governed. Since 1974 over a third of the republic's territory has been occupied by a foreign power, once again Turkey, and Turkish troops. This means that Turkey is a major factor in Cypriot domestic politics, shaping the policies of the legitimate government of Cyprus, which is forced to expend a great deal of energy trying to reunite

The Apollo temple at Koúrion dates from the Roman era

Cyprus. A UN peace force patrols the demarcation line Turkey has drawn across Cyprus by the use of force. Britain has two large bases on the island which are not under the jurisdiction of the Republic of Cyprus government. Cyprus will be unable to embark on a new chapter of its history until it becomes a full-fledged member of the EU. Negotiations on membership commenced in November 1998.

Irrigation

Like all Mediterranean islands, Cyprus suffers from water shortage. Steadily increasing numbers of tourists are exacerbating the problem. However, a solution may be at hand: during the six winter months there is enough precipitation in the mountains to provide the entire island with a year's supply of water. It just must be caught, stored and piped. Since 1960 many irrigation basins and reservoirs have been built and still more are under construction. Channels and pipelines take the water from the mountains all the way to Límassol, Lárnaka, Nicosía and Agía Nápa, where it irrigates crops and gurgles from taps. Work on additional reservoirs and conduits will not be completed until the next millennium. Until then, holidaymakers should use the island's precious water sparingly.

Byzantium

Byzantine art is everywhere in Cyprus. You visit Byzantine churches with their frescoes and icons, are confronted with the ruins of Byzantine forts and city fortification walls and never stop hearing about how Byzantine tradition lives on in music, folk art and the Cypriot mindset. The Byzantine double eagle still adorns most churches, symbolizing both the continuity of the Orthodox Church and the fall of the Byzantine Empire. Byzantium is the island's link with Greece, which sees itself as a direct descendant of Byzantium. Cyprus was never part of Greece, yet both Cyprus and Greece were part of the Byzantine Empire. The longing for reunification of all Greek Orthodoxy under the banner of Constantinople goes back 800 years. It has its roots in the conquest of Cyprus by Crusaders in 1191. For 250 years Cyprus strove for reunification with the Byzantine Empire, which lasted until 1453. When Greece threw off Turkish rule in 1828, Hellas replaced Byzantium as the symbol of Orthodox unity.

In AD 330 the Emperor Constantine transferred the capital of the Roman Empire from Rome to the Bosporus. In 395 Emperor Theodosius partitioned the Roman Empire. The city on the Bosporus, now called Constantinople, became the hub of the East Roman Empire. The Turks conquered Constantinople in 1453, renaming it Istanbul. Greeks from Mégara near Athens had founded it in 660 BC as Byzantion.

Rome and the West Roman Empire suffered repeated incursions and looting at the hands of the West Goths, the Vandals and the Huns, finally falling in AD 476. By contrast, the East Roman emperors managed to retain and even consolidate their imperial power.

Under Justinian I (527–565), the Byzantine Empire extended to Italy, North Africa, Spain and deep into Asia Minor. Cyprus was part of this Empire.

Orthodox Christianity was the state religion of the Byzantine Empire and Greek was its official language. When the Crusaders conquered Cyprus in 1191, Orthodox Christianity was degraded to the status of a second-class religion on the island and foreign languages were spoken at court. However, the Cypriots themselves never entirely broke off contact with Byzantium. The link with Byzantine tradition is what preserved Cypriot identity and kept the indigenous island culture, language and religion alive. Even Cypriot art reveals little Western influence. The conquerors in turn did not eschew Byzantine culture altogether. They commissioned Orthodox artisans to decorate their churches and even supported Orthodox monasteries. The cultural exchange between conquerors and the conquered proved stimulating for both sides, which is what makes the study of medieval Cypriot sacred art so rewarding.

Traditions established during the Byzantine era did not decline even after 1453. They were preserved by the churches, where they have maintained their influence to this day. Modern Orthodox ecclesiastical painting and architecture are rooted in this tradition. Orthodox divine service is celebrated according to the ancient liturgy.

Fauna

The only fairly large mammal living in the forests of the Tróodos is the Cypriot wild sheep, the moufflon. You're most likely to see one in the enclosure at Stavrós tis Psókas. The flocks of flamingos that spend the winter months on the salt lakes of Lárnaka and Akrotíri are probably the island's most exotic wildlife. Vultures, falcons and eagles are still occasionally seen in the mountains.

In summer sea turtles lay their eggs on the sandy beaches west of Páfos, where they are protected.

There are lots of lizards, but you'll rarely encounter snakes, even when you're on a long hike.

Flora

Cyprus is one of the most densely forested islands in the Mediterranean. A fifth of its surface area is once again covered with trees. Over thousands of years its forests were felled to build ships and houses and to supply charcoal for smelting and domestic heating. On the coasts olive and carob trees predomi-

nate. Tamarisks are the shrubs most frequently encountered on beaches and eucalyptus lines country roads. Cypress and acacias provide variety. In upland regions stands of Aleppo pine, holm oaks and poplar as well as nut and fruit orchards thrive. In the western outliers of the Tróodos, there are over 30,000 cedars. Above timberline mountains are covered with juniper and black pine.

The island's most important crop is grapes for wine and export. Grain grows mainly in the Mesaoría, the plain stretching between the two mountain ranges. A lot of citrus is cultivated on the north coast. Potatoes are grown in the Agía Nápa region and banana plantations surround Páfos.

In spring Cyprus is blanketed with flowers. The most common and spectacular wild flowers are asphodel and rock roses, hyacinths and narcissus, cyclamen and anemones, poppies, oleander and gorse as well as hibiscus and bougainvillea in gardens and on houses.

Gothic churches

It may seem surprising that the easternmost island in the Mediterranean boasts Gothic churches modelled on those of northern France. Yet there are two magnificent examples of this, the crowning achievement of medieval architecture, in Nicosía and Famagústa. The Lusignans had these churches built for their coronations in the 13th century. In the late 16th century the Turks had minarets added to them, but otherwise left them much as they were. The Gothic churches are certainly highlights of Cypriot architecture, blending beautifully with the island mosques and Byzantine churches.

The Green Line

Cyprus has been severed into two parts since 1974. A demarcation line 217 km long divides the Turkish-occupied north from the free part of the Republic of Cyprus, where the population is overwhelmingly Greek Cypriot. The old town of Nicosía was arbitrarily partitioned as early as 1964. A line that was simply drawn across the city map in green ink was from then on dubbed the Green Line. The name now denotes the entire demarcation line stretching across the island.

This arbitrary and unnatural border is today patrolled by soldiers representing three nations. On the north side Turkish and Turkish-Cypriot units are stationed; on the south Greek and Greek-Cypriots guard the Green Line. Between them runs a broad strip, from 10 m to 7 km wide, known as the Buffer Zone. It is patrolled by soldiers of the UNFICYP peace force, who are there to prevent clashes between the hostile parties and nip conflicts in the bud before they worsen. In addition, the UN troops ensure that the fields in the Buffer Zone can be peacefully cultivated by farmers on both sides.

Outside Nicosía watch towers and flags are all that make holidaymakers aware of the Green Line. It certainly doesn't threaten tourists in any way. In Nicosía the Green Line is marked by a simple low wall, which is reinforced with sandbags and empty oil drums painted blue and white. In some places the Green Line is simply identical with Nicosía's medieval city fortification wall.

Icons

Representations of saints and biblical events painted on panels are called icons in the Orthodox Church. They are plentiful in all churches and devout Orthodox Christians' homes. They even adorn the dashboards of public buses and the wheelhouses of fishing boats.

Unlike the devotional pictures in non-Orthodox churches, icons are more than just decorations. Bringing saints into churches and ensuring their spiritual presence, icons are the Gates of Heaven.

Therefore they are venerated, kissed, presented with gold and silver, jewels and elaborately embroidered curtains. Icons are Heaven's consulates on earth and as such are treated in every way as if they were the very saints themselves.

This is not idolatry. The icon is not venerated as an image; the saint represented is venerated as if actually present. An icon is regarded as ontologically identical with the saint depicted.

To ensure that this is so, icon painters, like the painters of frescoes in churches, must adhere strictly to an age-old aesthetic canon of established prototypes. Such painters have little scope for imagination and creativity. This is why so many icons look identical, regardless of whether they are modern or were painted centuries ago.

Archbishop and President: Makários III governed Cyprus for 17 years

However, Cypriot icon and fresco painters were exposed to Western pictorial art during centuries of foreign rule. Moreover, Franks and Venetians often commissioned artisans to paint icons recognizably in the Western manner. This dichotomy has left distinctive traces in Cypriot ecclesiastical painting, which deviates in some particulars from the austere formal Byzantine code. As far as content was concerned, however, Cypriot painters adhered strictly to the Byzantine canon.

The tradition of icon painting was established during and especially after Iconoclasm (726–843), when figurative religious images were officially banned. The issue of whether icons should be venerated at all sparked off an internecine war within the Byzantine Empire. By the time the advocates of icons finally prevailed, countless works of Early Christian art had been destroyed. From then on all figurative art had to be justified by its theological significance. This led to prescriptive art, bound by strict conventions, and the stringent canon that is still adhered to. The icon painters living on Cyprus certainly follow it. A visit to one of their workshops is a truly memorable experience.

Makários III

The archbishop who was head of state in the Republic of Cyprus for the first 17 years of its independence is still encountered in numerous photos adorning the walls of restaurants and hotels and in the form of monumental statues. Makários III was the Father of the Republic of Cyprus and his politics are rarely criticized. Born in 1913 to a peasant family in the Tróodos mountain village of Páno Panagiá, he was sent at the age of 11 by his recently widowed father to Kykko Monastery for his novitiate. The monastery paid for his schooling and theological studies. In 1948 he was annointed Bishop of Kítion (Lárnaka) and two years later Archbishop of the island.

From an early age Makários had been committed to ending British rule on the island and bringing about union with Greece. He became the political leader of Greek Cypriots, inspiring the armed struggle against colonialism with fiery oratory. It seemed only right that he should be elected the first President of the new republic in 1960. As President of the Republic of Cyprus, he retained his status as Archbishop of the island.

In the years that followed, Makários strove to limit the administrative, political and police powers that had been granted by the constitution to Turkish Cypriots. He countenanced military measures against Turkish Cypriots and, in so doing, exacerbated the political tensions on the island. His foreign policy consisted of a steadfast commitment to maintaining Cypriot neutrality and to reducing economic dependence on Great Britain.

When the colonels led a putsch in Greece in 1967 and established a dictatorship there, Makários distanced himself from the policy of Énosis, union with Greece. His condemnation of the military junta in Athens made its members his bitter foes. It was the colonels who plotted to overthrow him in 1974 but, after the Turkish invasion of Cyprus that same year, Makários was able to return to the island in December. Until his death in 1977, he governed only part of a divided island. Cypriots still flock to his tomb on a mountain near Kykko Monastery, which is a national shrine.

Religion

Nearly all Greek Cypriots profess the Greek Orthodox faith. The Cypriot Greek Orthodox Church is, however, independent of the Orthodox Church in Greece and far older. The Orthodox Church of Cyprus is, in fact, the oldest state church in Christendom.

The Early Christian Church was originally subdivided into five patriarchates: Rome, Constantinople, Alexandria, Antioch and Jerusalem. The patriarchs were the temporal and spiritual rulers of Christendom, transcending national and island boundaries. The Cypriots strove early on to detach their Church from the jurisdiction of the Patriarch of Antioch, justifying their claim to independence by recalling that the Apostle Barnabas had been the island's first bishop. By 477 Cyprus had achieved autocephaly, ecclesiastical autonomy, which Greece did not attain until 1850.

Holidaymakers are sure to notice Orthodox priests, whose appearance is certainly distinctive. They wear long dark ecclesiastical vestments, full beards and stove-pipe hats behind which a single plait of hair of some length emerges. They work like normal farmers in the fields, sell their produce at market and appear everywhere in public with their families. Orthodox priests marry before their ordination.

Greek Orthodox churches are as distinctive as their priests. Some are magnificently decorated with frescoes and are full of icons. Superb chandeliers hang from the ceilings. There is neither sculpture nor confessional, and even baptismal fonts are rarely fixed appointments in Orthodox churches.

Greek Orthodox divine service often lasts two or even three hours. During it men and women still stand or sit segregated from one another. Very few worshippers stay for the entire service. People are always coming and going. Members of the Orthodox congregation chat with each other and greet newcomers audibly. Sermons are almost unknown. The Greek Orthodox service consists of antiphonal responses sung by the priest and lay voices. The liturgy according to which service is celebrated changes daily, and there are no hymnals for the congregation.

Roman Catholic and Greek Orthodox practice differ noticeably in the way the sign of the Cross is made. Orthodox Christians cross themselves with only three fingers instead of all five. Another important Orthodox ritual is kissing the holy icons.

Orthodox Christians do not recognize the spiritual authority of the Pope as the Head of Christendom. They feel closer to the Apostles and the Early Christians because the tenets of their belief have hardly changed since the 8th century. They deplore both the Protestant Reformation and the new dogmas continually issued by the Pope as merely the work of man, heretical deviations from the True Faith. Uneducated Orthodox Christians may even regard Protestants and Catholics as just as pagan as they do Muslims and Hindus.

Orthodox doctrine does differ markedly from Roman Catholic dogma. The Schism in the Church took place in 1054 because the Orthodox Christians believed, as they still do, that the Holy Spirit emanates from God the Father only, whereas the Pope proclaimed that it issues from both Father and Son. Orthodox Christians do not believe in the Assumption of the Virgin; according to their teaching, Christ carried only her soul to heaven. Consequently, 15 August, one of the Orthodox high holy days, commemorates the Dormition, not the Assumption, of the Virgin.

Temples

You won't find temples like the ones familiar from Greece and southern Italy on Cyprus. The heyday of ancient Cyprus long predated the Athens Acropolis and ancient Cypriots worshipped their deities in sanctuaries like those known from the Near East. During the Roman era, the island was merely a minor Roman province so that no large temples were built on it then. The Apollo temple at Koúrion, which has been partly reconstructed, is the only one of its kind that might be said to match the expectations of visitors accustomed to classical archaeological sites.

Start off with a brandy sour

The national drink of Cyprus is a legacy of the British colonial era

Cypriots are enthusiastic eaters and drinkers. The island cuisine shows the influence of many cultures. Turkish, Oriental, Italian and British elements make it variegated and tasty. Only fresh local produce is used to make the national dishes you'll enjoy here.

Despite modern kitchen appliances, charcoal grills and traditional clay ovens are still widespread. Grills are used for fish and popular meat dishes like
soúvla – kebabs with pieces of meat the size of your fist;
skeftaliá – spicy pork sausages wrapped in lamb's belly;
brizóla – pork or veal cutlets;
paidákia – lamb chops;
halloúmi – firm sheep's milk cheese.
From the clay oven, *foúrnos* or *ófton,* come meat dishes like *kléftiko* – lamb or succulent kid roasted au jus with lemony potatoes.

Cypriot cooks also know how to conjure up mouth-watering

Even a quick road-side snack can be a great treat

specialities in conventional pots and pans:
afélia – marinated pork braised in red wine;
ravióles – large, cheese-filled ravioli;
stifádo – pork or beef stew with onions in a sauce seasoned liberally with cinnamon or sometimes cumin.
A Cypriot meal is always accompanied by salads and, for starters, dips of all kinds such as
humus – a thick paste made of chickpeas, oil, parsley and garlic;
melindsánosaláta – a thick paste of aubergines, mayonnaise or yoghurt, oil and garlic;
tachíni – a thick dip made of sesame, oil, garlic and lemon juice;
talatoúri – a dip resembling Greek *tzazíki* and consisting of yoghurt, oil, cucumber and garlic;
taramosaláta – a thick, creamy blend of cod roe and mashed potato.
Two delicious meat dishes, which are always served cold, are also specialities of Cypriot cuisine:

khiroméri – salt-cured goat's meat;
loúndsa – salt-cured chops.

All at a single sitting

It's easy to become acquainted with a wide variety of Cypriot delicacies at a single sitting. Almost all restaurants advertise what is known as *mezé* (which is pronounced mezé, not métse; the plural is *mezédes*). This is a spread of 12 to 20 different dishes served on tiny plates. You help yourself to whatever takes your fancy. You have the choice of meat, fish and vegetarian *mezé*.

Drinks

It goes without saying that a good wine goes well with a delicious meal on Cyprus. Until very recently, wine was the island's main export. You'll be amazed at the variety of wines on offer. However, these are table wines, not noble vintages. It's advisable to drink young two-year-old wines.

There are white, rosé and red wines, available in dry, semi-sweet and sweet. The dry white wines we recommend include Aphrodíti and Palamíno. Othéllo and Ermís are good reds. Rosélla and Amorósa, dry rosés, round off the palette of good Cypriot table wines that go well with meals and snacks.

Beer is also brewed on Cyprus. Two available brands are Kéo and imported Carlsberg.

Non-alcoholic beverages are available everywhere. Non-carbonated mineral water is called *metallikó neró*; carbonated mineral water is referred to as *sóda*.

Locally made sherry and ouzo make good aperitifs. If you like a little something after a meal, we recommend a bitter orange liqueur called *filfar*, a desert wine, *commandaría*, or a Cypriot brandy, which is popular during the winter months especially and is drunk like wine or beer in large quantity with meals. The best brandy is one called 'Five Kings'.

Brandy sour: quite a refreshing long drink, a legacy of British colonial rule, which has become the Cypriot national drink. It is made by combining one part Cypriot brandy with one part lemon or lime syrup followed by a dash of Angostura bitters and then the glass is filled up with soda. The rim of the glass is moistened and dipped in sugar. Nuts or raw carrot sticks are served with it. The best brandy sours of all are served at the Holiday Inn Hotel in Nicosía.

Hotel food

Cypriot hotel restaurants generally serve excellent food. Breakfast, of course, shows British influence. Sausages and eggs or omelettes are always on the breakfast buffet at the best hotels. Smaller hotels charge extra for English-style breakfasts.

At noon and in the evening hotels often serve Cypriot cuisine; many hotels offer buffets once or even several times a week. Hotel buffets are like ordering *mezé* at a restaurant; you just eat your way through a vast variety of Cypriot national delicacies.

Eating out

In cities and tourist centres you will be overwhelmed by the

The kafeníon is a local communications centre in Cyprus

number and diversity of restaurants to choose from. You will also find restaurants and *kafeníons* on country roads and in mountain villages. Outside the towns, eateries specialize in grilled food and *kléftiko*, lamb or kid roasted in a clay oven.

Restaurant menus are as a general rule written in both languages: Greek and English. Prices listed include a ten per cent service charge as well as three per cent VAT. Bread is always served with meals and is itemized on the bill, even though you may not have taken any from the basket.

Most restaurants are open from 12 noon to 3 pm and in the evening between about 7 pm and 11 pm. It is customary to reserve tables only for large parties, otherwise it is unnecessary.

Coffee houses and pastry shops

Pastry shops can only be found in cities. They are called *zakaroplastíon* and serve all sorts of alcoholic and non-alcoholic beverage (except wine) as well as puddings and Oriental pastries,

for example *baklavá* – layered fílo or puff pastry filled with ground almonds and drenched in sugar syrup; *gálatoboúreko* – puff or fílo pastry filled with vanilla pudding; *skamáli* – semolina with almond flakes sprinkled on top.

Coffee houses are as ubiquitous in towns and nearly all small villages as the *kafeníon* of Greek fame. On felt-covered tables cards, draughts and *távli* (backgammon) are played in *kafeníons*. Ouzo, brandy, beer, non-alcoholic beverages and coffee are served in them. Instant coffee, always called Nescafé, is often drunk cold, shaken like a cocktail and known as frappé. Greek coffee, mocha, is the usual drink, ordered as *kipriakó kafé* and made to your specifications, just as you like it:

skétto – without sugar
métrio – with a little sugar
varíglikó – very sweet, with a lot of sugar.

Mocha is never drunk with milk, but a glass of refreshingly cold water is always served with it.

Lefkarítika and leather goods

Folk art and Cypriot crafts make great souvenirs

Cyprus is not a paradise for souvenir hunters. The range of original souvenirs on the market is not all that wide. Folk art probably makes the best souvenirs.

Drawn-work embroidery, a precursor of lace, has been made for centuries in the village of Páno Léfkara and is available as table cloths and napkins, blouses and handkerchiefs. Genuine Lefkarítika drawn work is expensive. The cheap variety now available is from the Far East.

Lacy silver filigree work is also an attractive product made at Páno Léfkara and other villages by local craftsmen.

Little woven carpets and brightly coloured embroidery are for sale in many places. Leather goods are available only in cities. Much of the pottery sold was made at the village of Kórnos. Lovely handmade baskets are sold in Geroskípou and Liopétri. They are particularly cheap in city market halls. Wooden chairs with woven rush seats can be ordered

Genuine Páno Léfkara drawn-work lace is not cheap

from craftsmen in the mountain village of Finí.

Of course hand-painted icons are exceptional souvenirs. You can order them from the icon painters at Ágios Geórgios Alemánnos Monastery and Ágios Minás Convent but you will have to wait months before they can be finished and sent off to you.

If you're shopping for souvenirs, don't neglect the specialities for which Cyprus is deservedly renowned. Cypriot sherry, ouzo or brandy, *filfar* or *commandaría* are not readily available abroad. Drinking them will bring back happy holiday memories. While enjoying thyme honey, fruit preserves, sheep's milk cheese, *halloúmi*, or fruit jelly called in Greek *loukoúmia* or Turkish Delight in English, which is made at Geroskípou and Páno Léfkara, you can regale guests with tales of your holidays.

Shop and market opening hours

Mon – Sat 8 am – 1 pm,
Mon, Tues, Thurs, Fri 4 pm – 7 pm
(May – Sept), otherwise
2.30 pm – 5.30 pm (Oct – Apr)

Carnival and processions

Orthodox holy days are highlights of the Greek Cypriot festival calendar

NATIONAL HOLIDAYS

1 January *New Year's Day*
6 January *Epiphany Monday before Lent*
25 March *Greek Independence Day*
1 April *Cypriot national holiday*
Good Friday
Easter Sunday and Monday
1 May *Labour Day*
15 August *Feast of the Dormition*
1 October *Independence Day*
28 October *Greek national holiday*
24 December (afternoon);
25/26 December *Christmas*
31 December (afternoon) *New Year's Eve;*

Most shops and businesses are closed on national holidays. Museums and archaeological sites have special opening times on holidays, which you should enquire about upon your arrival so that you won't find the door shut in your face when you get there.

Cypriot festivals always had folk dancing but, unfortunately, it is now rarely seen except at special performances put on for tourists

MOVABLE FEASTS

The dates of movable feasts like Easter rarely coincide with Roman Catholic and Protestant ones as Orthodox holy days are not calculated according to the Gregorian but to the Julian calendar.

Carnival and Monday before Lent

★ The last week before Lent is colourful in the city of Límassol, with plenty of masquerading. Carnival parades inch through confetti-filled streets. Tavernas and hotels swing with riotous revelry and dancing. City dwellers drive out into the country for picnics on the Monday before Lent and in place of meat, which is standard fare all year round, fish, *halvás* and round loaves of bread, *kouloúria*, are eaten. *Monday before Lent: 2000 on 13 March, 2001 on 26 February, 2002 on 18 March*

Easter

★ During Holy Week divine service is celebrated in churches every evening before Easter. On the evening of Good Friday, the symbolic tomb of Christ is carried through the streets of towns and cities in processions. Afterwards an all-night wake is held in many churches beside the tomb. The Resurrection service begins late Saturday evening before Easter Sunday. On the dot of midnight, a shout of 'Christós anésti – Christ is risen' echoes through the churches, thousands of candles are lit and fireworks and crackers are set off. Afterwards, many restaurants serve Easter soup, *magirítsa*, to guests. On Easter Sunday Easter lambs and kid are grilled and enjoyed by family parties of Greek Orthodox Cypriots everywhere. *Easter Sunday: 2000 on 30 April, 2001 on 15 April, 2002 on 31 March*

Kataklismós

★ At all Greek Cypriot coastal towns and villages Whit Monday is celebrated as the Feast of the Deluge, Kataklismós, to commemorate the subsiding of the waters round Noah's ark. Lárnaka really takes this festival seriously. Along the promenade a fair is held from the weekend before Whitsun to the Tuesday after. There amateur dancers and musicians compete at music contests and poets and other artists present their work. Whit weekend also sees a spate of yachting regattas, surfing and water-skiing competitions. *Whit Monday/Kataklismós: 1999 on 31 May, 2000 on 19 June, 2001 on 4 June*

OTHER FEASTS & FESTIVALS

The helpful Cyprus Tourism Organization branch offices in Agía Nápa, Lárnaka, Límassol, Nicosía and Páfos can be depended on to bring you up to date and keep you informed on the following religious holidays and local festivals.

January
24 January: *Consecration feast* at Ágios Neófytos Monastery, Páfos.

February
2 February: *Consecration feast* at Panagías Chrysorrogiátissa Monastery near Páno Panagiá.

June

Mid-June: *Shakespeare Nights* in the ancient amphitheatre at Koúrion.

29 June: on the Feast of Saints Peter and Paul at Káto Páfos, a special *divine service* is celebrated, with congregations as well as the archbishop and all bishops of Cyprus taking part.

July

Early July: *International Culture Festival* with concerts and exhibitions in Límassol.

August

First week in August: *Folklore Festival* in Paralímni.

★ 15 August: the *Feast of the Dormition* is celebrated throughout the island with excursion parties of relatives, friends and acquaintances to beaches or the mountains. Mounds of meat are grilled at picnics and partying goes on non-stop. This is also the day numerous monasteries and churches celebrate their *consecration*, amongst them Panagías, Chrysorrogiátissa, Kykko, Machairás and Troodítissa.

September

Folklore Festival in Agía Nápa.

★ First to second weekend in September: *Wine Festival* in Límassol City Park. For a reasonable admission charge, you can drink as much wine as you can hold, made by Cypriot wine-producers, while you listen to Greek music and watch Cypriot folk dancing.

8 September: *Consecration feasts* at Kykko Monastery, the church at Asínou and at Lagouderá.

★ Mid-September: *Culture Festival* in Nicosía, with international orchestras, theatre groups and exhibitions as well as folklore and shadow-puppet performances.

13/14 September: *Consecration feasts* at Ómodos, Páno Léfkara and Stavrovouní Monastery.

October

4 October: *Consecration feast* at Kalopanagiótis.

Stavrovouní Monastery: mid-September is Consecration Feast

Wind farms and greenhouses

*Agriculture has left its stamp on the region between Lárnaka
and Agía Nápa*

Between the Tróodos Mountains, the Mesaoría plain and the sea, the country is hilly and rolling. Plains and low, usually bare, mesas are austerely beautiful but in summer and autumn may strike some as rather arid. The coasts of this region are fringed by the longest sandy beaches in Cyprus. The main city of the region is Lárnaka, which is challenging the ranking of even Agía Nápa as a tourist centre. Between Famagústa in the Turkish-occupied part of the Republic of Cyprus, yet barely 20 km

Agía Nápa: superb beaches make this a popular holiday resort

away as the crow flies, and Agía Nápa, a brand-new tourist centre is mushrooming. It is featured in travel agents' brochures as Protarás-Paralímni.

The inhabitants of this region live from tourism, a very important sector indeed of the local economy, and from the port and oil refineries at Lárnaka. Another major employer is Larnaca International Airport, which was built in just 40 days after the 1974 Turkish invasion of the north to serve a large catchment area.

The British soldiers and their families stationed at Dhekelía between Lárnaka and Agía Nápa play another important role in

---

Hotel and restaurant prices

Hotels

Category 1: CYP 65 – 150
Category 2: CYP 35 – 65
Category 3: CYP 14 – 35
Prices listed are for two people in a double room with breakfast (during peak season).

Restaurants

Category 1: over CYP 10
Category 2: CYP 7 – 10
Category 3: under CYP 7
Prices listed include a three-course meal (category 1) or a *mezé* spread (categories 2 and 3) without drinks.

the island economy. The local farmers between Lárnaka and Agía Nápa grow large, extremely tasty potatoes, which are also an export crop. In addition, olives, grain, melons, vegetables and even wine are cultivated here. Numerous wind farms at Agía Nápa provide the power for pumping ground water up to irrigate the fields. Greenhouse-grown early fruits, tomatoes and other vegetables as well as cut flowers are much in demand on both the domestic and international markets and consequently fetch premium prices.

AGÍA NÁPA

(109/E4) ★ In the south-eastern corner of the island, what was once a fishing village with barely a dozen small houses before the 1974 invasion has grown into one of the island's largest holiday resorts (pop. 2,500). Agía Nápa is a man-made city and is obviously still suffering from growing pains. Nevertheless, the urban planners who designed it have managed to avoid ruining the scenery with bulky high-rises. Hotels here fit into the coastal landscape with its sandy coves. The roads here are lined with rather small modern houses.

The only old building in Agía Nápa is its medieval monastery, round which the new town centre has sprung up. The fishing port is still idyllic, with views down an endless sandy beach fringed with low dunes and beach-front hotels. West of Agía Nápa there are sandy coves dotted with hotels and tavernas. Limpid blue water without surf make them ideal places for the whole family or lovers seeking solitude to swim and sunbathe. You can also swim out at Cape Gréco (Greek: Akrotírio Gréko).

Agía Nápa has everything for holidaymakers who want to swim, do water sports, eat well and dance the nights away. A drawback of the new town, which has a capacity of over 9,000 hotel beds, is that it's further away than any other place from the sights visitors shouldn't miss.

MARCO POLO SELECTION: AGÍA NÁPA & LÁRNAKA

SIGHTS

Hellenistic tombs
In the Hellenistic-Roman era, 19 tombs were hewn from the rock of the Makrónissos Peninsula. *Admission free*

Agía Nápa Monastery
Founded in about 1530, the monastery is today both a museum and an ecumenical conference centre. Admission standards are lax; latter-day goddesses sporting bikinis are even tolerated in the inner quadrangle, contrasting sharply with the austere Gothic architecture. The view from the cloister across the domed fountain and the massive gate tower is superb. A visit to the grotto chapel, still consecrated to Orthodox rites, can be a disappointment, though, if you're not prepared to accept kitsch icons. A boar's head gargoyle in the quadrangle goes back to Roman antiquity.

A huge sycamore has guarded the monastery south gate for over 400 years. The village church, consecrated in 1994 and decorated with frescoes throughout, stands below the monastery in the modern village square.

RESTAURANTS

Oleander
A taverna with open charcoal grill and children's menus, lots of ambience. *Daily from 6 pm, 10 Krió Neró Avenue, category 2*

Vassos Fish Harbour
A large, simply furnished old local taverna situated right on the fishing port. *Daily 11 am – midnight, category 3*

HOTELS

Grecian Bay
Large hotel with 240 rooms; freshwater swimming pool in the garden and an indoor pool; situated on a white sandy beach. Facilities for the disabled. *Tel. 03 / 72 13 01, Fax 72 13 07, category 1*

Kermia Beach
Bungalow park 4 km south of Agía Nápa with a beach highly suitable for children. Entirely self-catering. *154 rooms, Tel. 03 / 72 14 01, Fax 72 14 29, category 2*

SPORTS & BEACHES

There are beaches not only at Agía Nápa but also all along the west coast, extending to the north, east and west of town. You can reach them quickly by bicycle, moped or hire car. Excursion boats even land at some beaches. All larger beaches are good for surfing, paragliding, water-skiing and pedalo excursions. There are also several diving schools. However, visitors can enjoy the underwater scenery without getting wet by joining excursions in a glass-bottomed boat. The big pool complex *Waterworld*, a labyrinth of giant slides, is on the road to Agía Thékla *(follow road signs, Apr – Oct daily 10 am – 6 pm)*. Bungee-jumping facilities at Nissí Bay.

ENTERTAINMENT

Discos are terribly popular in Agía Nápa and there are lots of them. Hotel personnel and restaurant waiters invariably know which ones are 'in' at the moment.

Cyprus Tourism Organization
Tel. 03 / 72 17 96, 12 Krió Neró Avenue (near monastery)

Derínia (Deryneia) (109/D3)
⬆ From the little village hospital you have a clear view of Famagústa. The foreground is marred by the derelict hotels of Varóches (Varósha), which boasted a capacity of 16,000 beds when it was a booming tourist centre before the 1974 invasion.

**Cape Gréco
(Akrotírio Gréko)** (109/F5)
The south-east tip of the island is off limits because there is a military base on the cape. Nevertheless, it's a beautiful drive there. Excursions by boat to rocky coves and sandy beaches can be arranged. *8 km from Agía Nápa*

Liopétri (108-109/C-D4)
In summer and autumn you can watch basket-makers hard at work at their craft here. *14 km from Agía Nápa*

Paralímni (109/E3)
A big village with *kafeníons* and tavernas, well worth an excursion. Three churches, two observation towers and an open-air stage grace the large village square. *5 km from Agía Nápa*

Potamós tou Liopetríou (109/D5)
Fishing boats are moored in the mouth of a little river and taver-nas on the shore always have fresh fish on the menu. *12 km from Agía Nápa*

LÁRNAKA

(107/D-E5-6) Unlike Agía Nápa, which is only an hour away by bus, Lárnaka is a lively city (pop. 65,000), which has grown up over the centuries so that there are far more locals than holidaymakers in its streets. This is the centre of the Cypriot oil-refining industry. A wide sandy beach borders the promenade in the city centre. Here you can sit under palm trees in any one of the innumerable strand cafés and soak up the Mediterranean ambience. Behind the beach lies the old town with its narrow, traffic-choked shopping thoroughfare and the market hall. Around it is a belt of residential and commercial high-rises, most of them built in the past 20 years. To the west of the fishing port and to the east of the refinery docks begin more miles of sandy beach, which are also lined with hotels. The hinterland of Lárnaka is flat; weather conditions permitting, you can sometimes see the distinctive cone of Stavrovouní mountain and the foothills of the Tróodos from here.

Very little is left of the ancient city of Kíti, which stood on the site of modern Lárnaka from the early Bronze Age until the Early Christian era. In the Middle Ages the city was known mainly for its salt lake and its harbour. When Cyprus was under Turkish rule, the consulates of several foreign powers were located here.

SIGHTS

Ancient Kítion

The excavation site north-east of town is often under water. You can pick out city fortification walls, temple foundations and copper-working sites. *Mon – Fri 9 am – 2.30 pm and, except for July and Aug, also Thurs 3 pm – 6 pm, admission 75c, Makherás Street*

Fort

The fort at the western end of the promenade was built in 1625. Stone anchors, cannons and cannon balls are displayed in its pretty inner court. Finds from local archaeological excavations are exhibited inside. *Mon – Fri 9 am – 6 pm (May – Sept till 7.30 pm), admission 75c, Ankara Street (strand promenade)*

St Lazarus Church

The medieval name of the city derives from Lárnax, the Greek word for a type of gabled wooden or clay sarcophagus. Many sarcophagi have been found at Lárnaka. One of them, discovered in the 9th century, was inscribed with the name 'Lazarus', the man mentioned in the Bible. No one doubted in the least then that this must be the second and final earthly resting place of the man whom Christ raised from the dead.

The crypt in which Lazarus was finally laid to rest is still accessible to the public, just below the church altar. The little church museum situated in the north-western corner of the quadrangle boasts handsome icons and various early liturgical vessels. *Daily 8 am–12.30 and 3.30 pm–6.30 pm (Sept–Mar 2.30 pm–5 pm); admission to museum 20c, Ágios Lázaros Street*

Turkish Quarter

The old Turkish Quarter is just west of the fort. Here stands the city's most important mosque, now used by Arabs. A walk through the Quarter with its Turkish houses gives you some idea of Cyprus in the old days. Signs with Turkish names arouse nostalgia for the pre-1974 era, when the two cultures lived side by side.

MUSEUMS

District Museum (archaeological)

Finds from Lárnaka and Choirokoitía as well as the neighbouring villages of Pyla and Arsos, where there was an ancient Aphrodite sanctuary. *Mon –Fri 9 am – 2.30 pm, Thurs (except for July and Aug) also 3 pm– 6 pm, admission 75c, Kalogréon Square*

Natural History Museum

A tiny natural history museum established in 1993 in Lárnaka City Park. *Tues–Sun 10 am – 1 pm and 3 pm – 5 pm (Oct–May Tues– Sun 3 pm – 5 pm), admission 20c*

Pierides Collection

This remarkable private collection is exhibited in a handsome 19th-century mansion in town. It is particularly notable for its outstanding ceramics, ranging from Late Neolithic combed ware to medieval plates, jugs and beakers. The rich collection of vessels in the unique Cypriot Iron Age bichrome (black and purple), freefield style with reserved panels (7th century BC) is fascinating. One vessel bears a representation of what may be a Phoenician warrior with a spear in his left hand and an adze in his right. A sword is suspended from his belt. On another a man is shown seated in a chair while a third vessel boasts a stylized composition of a tree with flanking birds flying to it from both sides. *Mon – Fri 9 am – 1 pm and 3 pm– 6 pm, Sat 9 am – 1 pm (15 June– 30 Sept Mon – Sat 9 am – 1 pm and 4 pm–7 pm), admission CYP 1, 4 Zénonos Kitiéos Street*

Municipal Art Gallery

Exhibition of contemporary art in restored warehouses dating from 1881. *Tues – Fri 10 am – 1 pm and 4 pm – 6 pm (June– Sept 5 pm– 7 pm), Sat 10 am – 1 pm, Oct – May also Sun 10 am – 1 pm, admission free, Platía Evrópis*

RESTAURANTS

To Dichoro

Family-run taverna in a charmingly restored section of Lárnaka old town. *Daily 11 am – midnight, 8 Watkins Street, category 3*

Zephyros Beach Tavern

Taverna on the fishing port featuring specialities like squab, domestic rabbit and snails. *Daily 12 – 4 pm and 6 pm – midnight, Psarolímano, category 1*

SHOPPING

Heliotropio Gallery

Work by contemporary Greek and Cypriot painters shown and sold here. *3 Gríva Digení Avenue, Mon, Wed – Sat 11 am – 1 pm and 5 pm – 8 pm*

State Handicrafts Centre

This is where you can get an idea of the vast range of authentic Cypriot art and crafts available. *6 Kósma Lyssiótis Street*

HOTELS

Atrium Zenon Hotel Apartments

Modern, with flats in the city centre. *77 flats, Zénonos Kitiéos/ Pierídes Streets, Tel. 04 / 62 01 00, Fax 62 01 05, category 2*

Four Lanterns Sunotel

The city's oldest hotel dates from the colonial era. Recently renovated; located directly on the strand promenade. *56 rooms, 19 Athens Street, Tel. 04 / 65 20 11, Fax 62 60 12, category 2*

Pavion

✝ Unassuming guest house right in the old town. *10 rooms, 11 St Lazarus Square, Tel. 04 / 65 66 88, Fax 65 81 65, category 3*

SPORTS & BEACHES

If you don't want to use the city beach, which has fine sand but is often crowded, you can take a bus that runs every half hour from the Makris bus terminal in Demokratías Square to the long but narrow sandy beaches east and west of the city. Hotels there offer a wide variety of water sports.

ENTERTAINMENT

Art Café 1900

✪ Artists' café with lots of ambience not far from the Pierides Collection; occasionally live music. *Daily from 6 pm, 6 Stasinoú Street*

Black Turtle Tavern

✪ A taverna on the first floor of an old house near St Lazarus

Church. Wednesday, Friday and Saturday live music from 9.30 pm. *Open daily from 8 pm, 11 Mehmet Ali Street, category 2*

INFORMATION

Cyprus Tourism Organization
– *Larnaca Airport, Tel. 04/ 64 30 00*
– *Vasiléos Pávlou Square, Tel. 04/ 65 43 22*

SURROUNDING AREA

Hala Sultan Tekké   **(107/D6)**
★ This sacred building is located in a grove of date palms and cypresses on the salt lake near Lárnaka. Once the island's major Muslim shrine, now a popular photographic motif.

When the Arabs first invaded Cyprus in AD 647, a noble woman who had known the Prophet Mohammed personally came with them. She happened to fall from her mule and died on the spot where the mosque now stands. Her tomb here became a place of pilgrimage, which devout Muslims still remembered and flocked to visit when the Turks conquered the island in 1571. The Ottoman viceroy of Cyprus did not have the present mosque erected on the site until 1816. In later years hostel accommodation for pilgrims was added to the complex.

The mosque is austere. From the interior, which no one may enter wearing shoes, you go into an annexe, where the tomb of the woman venerated here is only just visible in the dim light. *Daily 7.30 am – 7.30 pm (Oct – May only until 6 pm), admission free, 7 km from Lárnaka*

Choirokoitía (Khirokitía)   **(114/B4)**
★ The best preserved of roughly 50 Late Neolithic settlements known to have existed on Cyprus is an astonishing sight. European and English-speaking visitors are amazed to find that people were living here 8,000 years ago in a village with houses on stone footings; there is nothing like this in northern and western Europe.

The settlement was protected from enemy attack by a sort of fortification wall. Remains of it are easy to spot along the path leading uphill across from the settlement.

The houses were round and built close together. The settlement may have had a population of roughly 1,000 in a community like an extended family. The houses were of varying sizes; the biggest had a diameter of nearly ten metres. The walls were up to three metres thick. In some larger houses stone pillars suggest there were wooden platforms below the ceiling.

The houses were built of clay and sun-dried mudbrick on stone footings, which are still *in situ*. To show what these houses may have looked like, archaeologists have completely reconstructed four dwellings near the gate to the settlement.

Archaeologists found skeletons under the floors of several of the houses, each covered by a heavy stone. Perhaps the living feared that the dead would return to haunt them. Bones and remains of food were found, which give clues as to what these people who lived 8,000 years ago ate every day. Their diet was varied, consisting of pork, mutton, goat and venison, mussels, fish and crabs, pistachio nuts, figs, olives, barley, wheat, lentils and peas. *Mon – Fri 9 am – 6 pm (May – Oct until 7.30 pm), Sat and Sun 9 am – 5 pm, admission 75c, 31 km from Lárnaka*

Kíti (115/F4)

Huge terebinth (mastic: gum) trees shade the attractively paved square of this tiny village in which the Panagía Angelóktistos church stands, the 'all-hallowed church built by angels'. The building is eclectic, consisting of a Gothic Crusader chapel and a Byzantine church built to replace an Early Christian basilica. The apse vault of the basilica was decorated with a superb ★ mosaic, a masterpiece that was incorporated into the church built in the 10th century.

In brilliant colours glowing against a gold ground, the magnificent mosaic is a representation of the Virgin holding the infant Christ, enthroned on a pedestal set with gems and flanked by approaching archangels. Each brings an orb crowned with a cross to the Christ child. These spheres presumably cannot represent the orb of the world, which was still thought to be flat, although they are often thus interpreted. Here the sphere probably symbolizes perfection. Each angel carries a caduceus, a messenger's staff. Their robes are a swirl of elegance and their wings are composed of irridescent peacock feathers. The representation is framed by a border of stylized leaves and flowers, ducks, stags and parrots and vases with a centred cross. *Mon – Sat 8 am – 4 pm, Sun 9 am – 12 and 2 pm – 4 pm, admission free, 12 km from Lárnaka*

Ágios Minás Convent (114/B4)

★ The convent, which is rather like a fortress, is situated in a mountain valley ringed with peaks. Most of the icons hanging in the 18th-century convent church are new and were painted by the nuns themselves. You can even watch a nun painting icons in a first-floor room of the cell tract. She accepts orders for icons but you'll have to wait several months to receive your icon by post. *Daily 8 am – 12 and 3 pm – 7 pm. Women must wear skirts; admission free, 45 km from Lárnaka*

Stavrovouní Monastery (106/B6)

★ Don't forget: women are not admitted to this monastery! The island's oldest monastery perches atop a distinctively conical mountain rising from the coastal plain to an elevation of 768 m. A tortuous paved road winds almost to the top, affording superb views across the plain to the mountains and the sea.

The present buildings date from the 17th/18th centuries. A splinter of the True Cross is said to have been worked into the silver-mounted cross, which hangs to the right of the iconostasis.

Agía Varvára Monastery, right on the paved road at the foot of the conical mountain, also belongs to Stavrovouní and is economically productive. The monks keep bees and the honey here is outstanding. Across from this monastery is the workshop of Kallinikós, a monk who paints icons. *Agía Varvára Monastery is open to the public daily; only men may visit Stavrovouní daily 8 am – 12 and 3 pm – 6 pm (Sept– Mar 2 pm – 5 pm), 34 km from Lárnaka*

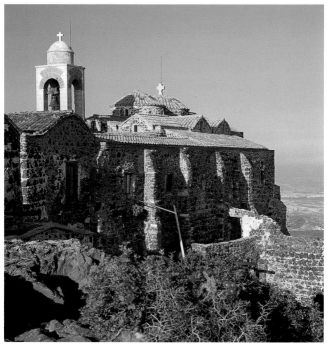

Stavrovouní, situated 768 m above sea level, is the oldest monastery on Cyprus

Páno Léfkara   **(114/B3)**

This large village in the Tróodos foothills is famous for drawn work, *Lefkarítika*, a precursor of real lace. Needlework of this kind and filigree silver jewellery are sold in the village. It's a good idea to enjoy a quiet walk through the narrow alleys of the town and to visit the needlework and jewellery museum before concentrating on the drawn work in the shops *(Mon – Thurs 9.30 am – 4 pm, Fri and Sat 10 am – 4 pm, admission 75c), 38 km from Lárnaka*

Pyrgá   **(106/B5)**

Next to the modern village church there is an early 15th-century medieval chapel with frescoes that are obviously in the Byzantine tradition yet must have been commissioned by Roman Catholic donors and executed to their taste. The inscriptions, for instance, are in Latin letters. You can get the key to what is popularly called the *Royal Chapel* in the *kafeníon* across from it. *21 km from Lárnaka*

Salt lake   **(107/D– E6)**

The salt lake at Lárnaka is a magnet for flamingoes in winter but dries up to a salt pan in summer. Rains fill the lake again with water for the six winter months. *On the outskirts of Lárnaka*

The perfect base for day trips

Límassol is centrally located for sightseeing excursions on Cyprus

Límassol (Greek: Lemesós) is centrally located on the south coast of Cyprus. Behind the coastal plain rise the outliers of the Tróodos Mountains. Mount Ólympos, the island's highest peak, is visible on clear days. The coast near Límassol is flat but to the east and west it is rocky and steep. From here the Akrotíri Peninsula juts far out into the sea. Still largely under British jurisdiction, the peninsula is the site of a military airport. The second largest salt lake on Cyprus dots the neck of the Akrotíri Peninsula.

The coastal strip round Límassol is fertile. Wine and numerous fruit crops are grown here. Fruit juice and canned fruit are made in several small processing plants in and near Límassol.

LÍMASSOL

(113/D-E 4-5) Límassol (Lemesós) the island's second largest city

Wine is grown in the fertile country round Kolóssi Castle

(pop. 146,000), is a buzzing modern metropolis that is showing signs of urban sprawl. The old town is insignificant compared with Nicosía's and is even fading as a shopping centre. Límassol is a much more bustling city than either Nicosía or Lárnaka. However it lacks the strand promenade and beach right at the centre of town, which make Lárnaka such an attractive holiday resort. Unlike Lárnaka or Páfos, Límassol doesn't have much to offer in the way of historic buildings or ancient monuments since Límassol was not founded until the Middle Ages. Earthquakes in 1567 and 1584 flattened almost all earlier buildings.

Most of the modern Cypriot wine producers are located in Límassol. Beer is brewed here as well and local distilleries make ouzo, brandy and liqueurs. Límassol harbour is the island's main port. Ships of all flags lying at anchor outside the harbour are an everyday sight here. Tourism centres on the coast just east of the city, where, unfortunately, there are very

41

few beaches. Hotel premises with pools compensate visitors for this lack. What is also of major importance for the economy of the Republic of Cyprus is a heavy concentration of international businesses and banks. Many of them were forced to move their Near East headquarters to Cyprus when civil war broke out in Lebanon.

Its central location makes Límassol the perfect base for holidaymakers who enjoy taking lots of day trips. Visitors who want to bask on the beaches and swim in the sea are far better off at Lárnaka and Agía Nápa.

SIGHTS

City park and zoo
The city park boasts a small zoo, which may not be up to Central European standards, but nature-lovers still shouldn't miss it. This is probably the only chance you'll have of seeing the Cypriot wild sheep, the famous moufflon. *On the coast road*

Wine producers
★ The four biggest Límasssol cooperative wine producers, KEO, SODAP, ETKO and LOEL, as well as the Keo Brewery are open to the public in the morning. To find out when, ask at your hotel or the Cyprus Tourism Organization. *The wine cooperatives are on the road between the centre and the port*

MUSEUMS

District Museum (archaeological)
This small museum, perhaps only interesting to archaeologists and archaeology aficionados, displays minor finds from excavations in Límassol district. *Mon – Fri 7.30 am – 5 pm, Sat 9 am – 5 pm, Sun 10 am – 1 pm, admission 75c, intersection Cannings/Byron Streets*

Ethnographic Museum
Six rooms of this building, erected in 1924, are filled with interesting implements and utensils, costumes, furnishings and crafts dating from several centuries as well as the first half of the 20th century. *Mon – Fri 8.30 am – 1.30 pm, Mon, Tues, Wed, Fri also 3 pm – 5.30 pm (June– Sept 4 pm – 6.30 pm), admission 30c, 253 Agios Andréas Street*

Museum of Medieval Cyprus
◁◁▷ A 14th-century castle houses tombstones, armour and weapons displayed with fascinating photographs of Cypriot medieval buildings. The roof affords a superb panoramic view across Límassol. *Mon – Sat 9 am – 5 pm, Sun 10 am – 1 pm, admission CYP 1, Irínis Street*

RESTAURANTS

Fiesta
Superb steaks; also definitely recommended for good *mezé*. ◁◁▷ Lovely sea-view terrace; the perfect place to relax. *Potamós Germasogías, George A' Avenue (500 m east of Apollonia Beach Hotel), category 2*

Ladas Old Harbour
A typical taverna famous for years for its delicious seafood, on the old port at the western end of the coast road. *Mon–Sat from 12 noon, Agías Théklis Street, category 1*

MARCO POLO SELECTION: LÍMASSOL

1 Market halls
Cypriot delicacies on sale here (page 43)

2 Wine cellars and brewery
Sample both wine and beer (page 42)

3 Koúrion
Amphitheatre with a sea view (page 46)

4 Fasoúri
Cypress tunnel through plantations (page 44)

5 Kolóssi
A castle where sugar was made (page 45)

6 Bunch of Grapes Inn
The island's most charming hotel in Pissoúri (page 47)

Nitayia

A sparkling restaurant on the Old Harbour serving Chinese, Thai and Japanese cuisine. *Daily from 5 pm, Agía Théklis Street, category 2*

The Old Neighbourhood

❂ An unpretentious, unspoilt little traditional taverna in the old town with excellent home cooking that draws many locals. They also have live music on many evenings. *Daily from 6 pm, 14 Odós ángyras (Ankaras), category 3*

SHOPPING

Market halls

★ The island's biggest and most picturesque market. Fish and meat, fruit and vegetables as well as hand-woven baskets and live domestic animals are sold here together with numerous Cypriot specialities. *Between Kanáris and Athens Streets*

State Handicrafts Centre

All the island's crafts at a glance. *25 Thémidos Street*

HOTELS

Aquamarina

Modern hotel, on the coast road, at the edge of the old town. *70 rooms, 139 Spyrou Araoúzou Avenue, Tel. 05 / 374277, Fax 374086, category 2*

Hawai Beach

Luxury hotel, 255 rooms, pool, beach. Facilities for the disabled. *Old Lefkosía-Lemesós Raod, Amathoús Area, Tel. 05 / 31 13 33, Fax 31 18 88, category 1*

Luxor

♟ Unpretentious guest house in the main old-town shopping street. *15 rooms, 101 Ágios Andréas Street, Tel. 05 / 36 22 65, category 3*

SPORTS & BEACHES

Only the locals swim in the sea off Límassol. Hotels to the west of town have small sandy beaches and they offer a wide range of water sports. Lady Mile Beach, Koúrion Beach and Governor's Beach are by far the most inviting places to swim in the area.

The beach hotels at Límassol are set in lush gardens

ENTERTAINMENT

Edó Lemesós
Top-quality *mezé* with authentic live Greek music. *111 Irínis Street, category 1*

Kyrenia Tavern
A big taverna with folklore shows on Wednesdays and live *bouzoúki* Fridays, Saturdays and Sundays. *Zakákia, Franklin Roosevelt Avenue, category 1*

INFORMATION

Cyprus Tourism Organization
15 Spyrou Araoúzou Avenue (Old Harbour), Tel. 05 / 36 27 56
35 George A' Street, Germasógia (hotel section), Tel. 05 / 32 32 11

SURROUNDING AREA

Ancient Amathoús (113/E4)
In Greco-Roman antiquity the city-kingdom of Amathoús was on the site of parts of the modern hotel section. Like ancient Kíti, where Lárnaka now is, Amathoús was not hellenized until the middle of the 1st millennium BC, when it ceased to be under Phoenician sway.

Hardly anything is left of the ancient city of Amathoús. East of the Amathus Beach Hotel you can visit the ruins of an Early Christian basilica on the left-hand side of the road. *Daily 7.30 am – 5 pm (May – Oct until 7 pm), admission 75c, 9 km from Límassol*

Fasoúri (112/C5)
★ The countryside south-west of Límassol is chequered with lush plantations. The road past them runs for miles through intertwined and overarching cypresses. Hedges protect lemon, orange and grapefruit groves; in recent years plantation owners have been experimenting with ventures into more exotic and lucrative crops like avocados and

kiwis. You can't walk in the plantations, but driving through the cypress tunnel is an experience you'll never forget. *5 – 10 km from Límassol*

Kolóssi (112/C4)

★ Kolóssi Castle rises up amongst the cypresses, a tawny fortress on the north-western fringe of the fruit plantations. Its roof affords superb views across the green oasis to the sea, the Tróodos and the modern highrises of Límassol.

Kolóssi Castle was built by the Knights of the Order of St John of Jerusalem. During the Crusades they cared for the sick and wounded in the Holy Land and on all pilgrimage routes. When the Lusignans conquered Cyprus, they sought allies to help their much smaller land forces guard against enemy attack. The Crusader orders and in particular the Knights of St John of Jerusalem were ideal for the purpose. The order was given Kolóssi and its domain, which included 60 villages and the people in them. After they were expelled from Palestine by the Arabs in 1291, the Knights of St John used the castle and its lands as an 'outpost' of their order, which they used as a tempo-

rary headquarters before moving to Rhodes in 1309. From there they continued to administer their Cypriot domain.

Kolóssi Castle was the residence of the viceroy of Cyprus and also the seat of the administrative offices of the domain. Wine and sugar cane were the principal crops cultivated there. A heavy sweet wine, known as Commandaría and still produced in the region, was made from grapes grown at Kolóssi. Sugar made from Kolóssi cane was exported to Venice.

The castle keep is just as it was in the late 15th century, although little is left of the wall surrounding it. Provisions for the castle and its occupants were

Kolóssi Castle, built by the Knights of St John

Achilles on Skíros

Knowing that Achilles would die in the battle for Troy, his mother hid her boy, dressed as a girl, in the palace of the king of Skíros. The Greek hero Odysseus realized that the Greeks could only take Troy if Achilles fought with them. Disguised as a pedlar, he went to Skíros and spread out his wares to tempt the girls in the palace, but included some weapons as well. Then he had a war trumpet sound. One of the girls at once snatched up a sword, revealing herself to be Achilles in disguise.

stored in the keep cellars, where there were cisterns to hold rainwater. The knights lived and worked in the two upper storeys.

A medieval aqueduct comes to an end at a huge, spreading maguey or Spanish bayonet tree growing on the east façade of the castle keep. Water conveyed to Kolóssi Castle via the aqueduct drove the millstones that ground the sugar cane. The sugar was actually made and processed in the elongated shed nearby. *Daily 9 am – 7.30 pm (Oct – May only until 5pm), admission 75¢, 12 km from Límassol*

Kourion (112/B4–5)

ᐱ⁄ᐱ Near Páfos, this archaeological excavation site is the most rewarding to visit on the south coast and extends across a plateau west of Límassol. In this lovely setting an amphitheatre, thermae (Roman baths), mosaic floors, the foundations of numerous urban buildings and dwellings, a stadium and a large Apollo sanctuary vie with the still impressive ruins of a grand Early Christian basilica for visitors' attention.

Called Curium by the Romans during their tenure there, the city existed by the early 1st millennium BC. What you see at Koúrion today, however, dates almost entirely from the Roman and even the Early Christian eras, that is, from the first six centuries of our era.

The best thing for you to start with is the *Sanctuary of Apollo Hylates* on what used to be the western edge of the city. The god was venerated here as the patron of woods and wild animals. In the sacred precincts you can see sev-

eral votaries' hostels, the priests' quarters and Roman thermae as well as a temple dating from the 1st century AD, which has been partly reconstructed. To the left of the Sacred Way, which leads to the temple façade, there is a rocky round with several noticeable depressions behind a wire fence. In these pits votaries of Apollo planted trees and danced in veneration of the forest divinity.

On the way back from the sanctuary to Límassol and the centre of ancient Koúrion via the main road, you pass what is recognizably a *stadium* dating from Roman times. Not much of its seven tiers of seats has been restored, but it once held roughly 6,000 spectators.

At the excavation site of the ancient city of Koúrion, start off with the ★ *amphitheatre*, which was laid out to look as it does today in the 2nd century AD and held 3,500 spectators. The view from the tiers of seats across the beach at Koúrion and the Akrotíri Peninsula is magnificent.

Next to the theatre you shouldn't miss the *mosaics in the House of Eustólios* before going on. They are particularly interesting to archaeologists because they date from the Christian era, i.e. the early 5th century AD. At that time representations of birds and geometric patterns were much more common than those of biblical scenes and saints like the ones you see here. Christ is named in inscriptions on the floor. The only depiction of a human figure is a female allegorical personification of 'Ktísis', which, translated, means creative powers. She holds a unit of measurement (the Roman 'foot') in her hand.

Like most of these mosaics, the impressive *large basilica* at the far end of the Koúrion excavation site is from the 5th century AD, that is, it dates from the era when pagan Koúrion was making the transition to Christianity. With its five aisles, the basilica must have been on an incredibly grand scale and superbly appointed, as remains of floor mosaics, roof tiles and the fountains in its two porches indicate. A small baptistery was built abutting the basilica to the north and the cruciform font in it has been preserved. Early Christians, like Orthodox Christians to this day, were completely immersed at baptism. However, in the 5th century, most people converted to Christianity, and were baptized as adults and that is why Early Christian fonts tend to look the way this one does.

Across from the basilica extends a vast expanse of ruins, once the *Acropolis*, or, so to speak, the inner city of ancient Koúrion. There is a tangle of foundation walls and the ruins of thermae with a fountain or nymphaeum. Near the fence and the main road there are three Roman mosaics *in situ*. One is a two-panel representation of gladiatorial combat. Another depicts the abduction of Ganymede by Zeus in the form of an eagle and a third shows Achilles being hidden by his mother, Thetis, on the island of Skíros. *Daily 7.30 am – 7.30 pm (Oct – May until 5 pm), admission to Apollo Sanctuary CYP 1, Koúrion 75c, 15 km from Límassol*

Lánia (112/C2)

Below this almost untouched village, directly on the main road from Límassol up into the Tróodos Mountains, is the *Royal Oak Café*, where you can even perch in the vast trunk of a centuries-old Portuguese oak. There are several craftsmen's shops in the village. *25 km from Límassol*

Pissoúri (111/E4 and F5)

Cyprus boasts fine hotels but scarcely any unconventional ones. The ★ *Bunch of Grapes Inn (Tel. 05 / 22 12 75, Fax 22 25 10, hotel category 3, restaurant category 2)* at Pissoúri, a mountain village near the coast, is a delightful exception. An old stone building, it was once a farmhouse. Its 11 rooms for guests open on to a romantic inner court, which is used in summer as a bar and restaurant. Guests who don't stay in the hotel can soak up the atmosphere of the courtyard.

Four km below the village the Columbia Pissouri Beach Hotel and several tavernas are right on Pissoúri's sand and pebble beach. *38 km from Límassol*

Yermasóyia (Germasógeia) (113/E3–4)

☙ This large village above the Límassol hotel section is not sought out by day trippers travelling round the island. Still it makes a pleasant change for visitors staying in Límassol. Here you see village life and can treat yourself to lavish *mezé* in a taverna, the *Flogera Tavern (8 pm – 1 am)*, where *bouzoúki* players go from table to table. *9 km from Límassol*

A capital divided

Nicosía (Lefkosía) is bisected by the Green Line
separating the Turkish-occupied part
of the Republic from free Cyprus

Over a quarter of all Cypriots live in and near Nicosía. At the centre of the Mesaoría plain, the city is bounded by the Kyrénia Mountains in the north, the Tróodos to the south-west and low, mesa-like outliers of the Tróodos to the south-east. The peaks of the Kyrénia Mountains and the Tróodos, whose deceptive roundness belies their height, are visible from the island capital on many days of the year.

Its favourable location in the plain has allowed Nicosía to sprawl. The city offers a great deal of employment in government and administration, commerce, the service sector and in industry. Roughly half of all Cypriot manufacturing goes on in greater Nicosía. The main goods produced are shoes, textiles and paper. Tourism doesn't play much of a role in and near Nicosía. Most holidaymakers only take day trips from the coast resorts to come here, mindful of the fact that the land-locked capital is always two to three degrees hotter than where they are staying. The residents of Nicosía also flee the capital's sweltering heat on summer evenings and Sundays to cool off by the sea or in shady mountain villages.

A sprawling growth of suburbs round Nicosía is rapidly expanding to house commuters who work in the city but prefer not to live there. However, the fertile plain is still intensively cultivated. The main crops grown here are wheat and barley.

The slopes of the Tróodos are largely wooded. There are some villages up there as well as monasteries, where monks and nuns still live and some interesting churches, which are easiest to visit if you're based in Nicosía.

NICOSÍA

☛ **City Map inside back cover**

(105/E–F1–2) A day might be just enough to enable you to become somewhat acquainted with Nicosía (pop. 189,000). Of course, if you want to become more familiar with the city and visit the sights nearby, you should plan to spend at least two or even three

The old town of Nicosía
does not stop at the city wall

nights here. Then you'd be able to explore the Turkish-occupied part of the old town on foot at your leisure. The Green Line runs straight through the Mesaoría, arbitrarily severing the Republic of Cyprus and Nicosía. Foreign visitors may cross it at only one checkpoint in the island capital.

Nicosía is over 3,000 years old, yet the city was of minor importance in antiquity. Far richer and more influential were Tamassós, renowned for copper mines and smelters (near modern Politikó) and Idalíon (now Dháli), which boasts an Aphrodite sanctuary. Nicosía is first mentioned in the 7th century BC in the records of Cypriot city-kingdoms, which were forced to pay tribute to the Assyrians. Then it was called Lédra. In the 3rd century BC it was founded again by Léfkos, a Ptolemaic prince, and renamed Lefkosía. Salamís enveloped the city in the 6th century. The city did not become the capital of the island until 1192, when the Lusignans gave it this status and named it Nicosía. Greeks call it Lefkosía and to Turks it's Lefkosha.

Nicosía is really a city twice divided. From any high vantage point you can easily spot the five-kilometre-long fortification wall with its striking bastions, which encloses the old town and its little houses spiked by the occasional church tower or minaret. Modern Nicosía has grown up around the walled old town, exuberantly to the south but reticently in the Turkish-occupied north.

The demarcation line between the Turkish-occupied north and south runs right through the old town of Nicosía. It is marked by a wall, reinforced with sandbags and empty oil drums. In places house façades mark the border.

The old town on both sides of the line is the only interesting part of Nicosía for many visitors. This is where the majority of museums are and certainly all historic monuments worth visiting. The main shopping thoroughfares, Lédra and Onásgoras Streets, are throbbing with life. The part of the old town known as Laikí Gitoniá is a great place to spend the evening. The new part of the city, however, which is bisected by Makários and Evágoras Avenues, is not particularly distinctive so you needn't feel concerned about missing it. You can see the attractively austere government buildings and ministries from your car or a city bus.

SIGHTS

Ágios Ioánnis Cathedral   (U/E4)
The city's Orthodox cathedral is surprisingly small and was built in 1662 on the foundations of a ruined Crusader church. The cathedral interior was lavishly decorated with frescoes between 1736 and 1755.

The representation of the Crucifixion is particularly striking. In its liveliness and wealth of figures it recalls typical Western painting, yet all major theological statements prescribed by the traditional Byzantine canon are included in it. Blood trickles from all the wounds on the feet of the Crucified onto Adam's skull to show that, through Christ's intercession, the dead will be resurrected. An angel hovers to catch the blood in a chalice, a reference to the Last Supper. Sun and moon, both painted with faces, proclaim that the Crucified is the ruler of the universe. An interesting narrative element is represented by the soldiers at the right-hand lower edge of the fresco. They are pointedly depicted wearing the Turkish dress typical of the time when the work was executed.

The representation of Judgement Day is also highly expressive in unusual detail. The Devil is shown on the right-hand lower edge of the fresco holding the treacherous Judas on his lap and, between his legs, beautiful Salome, whose mother forced Herod to have John the Baptist beheaded.

Depictions of the first seven ecumenical Councils at the rear of the church are to remind devout Orthodox Christians not to deviate from the doctrines which were proclaimed at them.

The historical event that led to the founding of the Cypriot national church is narrated in four panels on the right-hand wall, next to the Archbishop's throne. Barnabas the Apostle appears to Bishop Anthémios in a dream, disclosing to him where his grave is. Anthémios goes to the place revealed, where he finds the Apostle's corpse untouched by the ravages of death, with the Gospel according to St Mark in its hand. Anthémios presents the Gospel to the Byzantine Emperor Zenon at Constantinople and receives in exchange the insignia of an Archbishop of Cyprus: a scepter, a purple robe and red ink. *Mon – Sat 8 am – 12 noon and 2 pm – 4 pm, admission free, Archbishop Kiprianós Square*

Archbishop's Palace (U/E4)

When Cyprus became independent in the year 1960, Makários III had a spacious palace built in the old town. He resided there until 1977 as Archbishop and Head of State. A monumental statue of him still stands before this impressioned palace, where the present Archbishop, called Chrysóstomos, resides. The pres-

---

MARCO POLO TIP: NICOSÍA

1 Cyprus Museum
The treasures of antiquity assembled (page 54)

2 Selimiye Mosque
The muezzin's cry and Gothic architecture in the occupied part of Nicosía (page 60)

3 Laikí Gitoniá
Romantic atmosphere and good food in the old town (page 52)

4 Xefoto Taverna
Good food, great ambience and live Greek music in the evening (page 56)

5 Icon Museum
The most precious icons from Cypriot churches (page 54)

6 Asínou
900-year-old frescoes: a UNESCO World Cultural Heritage site (page 58)

ident of the Republic of Cyprus, however, is content with a much more modest house in the new part of the city. *Not open to the public, Archbishop Kiprianós Square*

Famagústa Gate (U/F4)

This handsomely restored Venetian city gate is today a municipal cultural centre, where lectures, exhibitions, concerts and theatre performances are held. The gate, which was called by the Venetians Porta Giuliana, is a 35-metre-long passage through the thick fortification wall connecting the old town of Nicosía inside with the outer moat. The old Venetian guardrooms used to line the passage. *Mon – Fri 10 am – 1 pm and 4 pm –* 7 pm (Aug 5 pm – 8 pm), Nikifóros Phókas Avenue*

Liberation Monument (U/E-F5)

The modern monument on the city wall across from the new Archbishop's Palace commemorates the liberation of the island from British colonial rule by EOKA freedom fighters. It is surmounted by a statue that depicts an allegorical personification of liberty. *Nikifóros Phókas Avenue*

Laikí Gitoniá (U/C5)

★ Quite a few of the old town houses are in dire need of restoration. In a central section of the old town, the city of Nicosía has undertaken renovation and restoration work: in Laikí Gitoniá,

Laikí Gitoniá: authentic Mediterranean ambience

52

the Old Neighbourhood. Since 1984 this has been a romantic spot with several tavernas in keeping with the atmosphere of the place and some souvenir shops. This is where you will find the Mediterranean ambience you've been longing for. *Between Regaena and Hippócrates Streets*

Maronite Quarter   (U/B4)

❖ The Maronites are a Christian community whose homeland is Lebanon. About 7,000 Maronites live in Cyprus. Since their ancestors came here a long time ago, Cypriot Maronites speak Greek as their mother tongue and are citizens of the Republic of Cyprus. The Maronite Church is linked to the Roman Catholic Church and recognizes the authority of the Pope as the head of their Church.

The quarter of the city where Cypriot Maronites have traditionally lived is in the western part of the old town. Their bishop's church stands here. Its façade and apse are decorated with new mosaics, which recall Byzantine tradition, yet bear Latin inscriptions. The interior of the church is austere and without the iconostasis familiar from Orthodox churches. Unlike them, the Maronite church also has sacred sculpture on the walls. *Key in bishop's office next to the church, between Arsínoe and Páfos Streets*

City walls

The city wall dates from the era of Venetian rule. A road runs along the top of lengthy sections of it. Reinforcedby 11 spectacular bastions, it originally had only three gates: the Famagústa (**U/F4**) and Páfos Gates (**U/B4**) in the west and the Kyrénia Gate (**U/C1**) in the north. The broad moat round the wall still exists, although different sports facilities and parking spaces fill much of it.

MUSEUMS

Cyprus Jewellery Museum   (U/C5)

Old jewellery and implements are shown here. *Laikí Gitoniá, Mon – Fri 10 am – 4.30 pm, admission free*

Ethnographic Museum   (U/E4)

The old Archiepiscopal Palace, where Makários III resided until 1960, houses the Ethnographic Museum. Much of the building dates from the Crusades, when it was erected as a Benedictine monstery. Part of the museum incorporates the old cloister. The focus of the collections is on pre-industrial implements and utensils. Folklore is represented by costumes, textiles, drawn work from Léfkara, handsome carved chests, jewellery and household furnishings and utensils. The collections also include icons and naive paintings by Kashialós, a self-taught artist. One of his works gives you a good idea of what a traditional village wedding was like. *Mon – Fri 9 am – 5 pm, Sat 10 am – 1 pm, admission CYP 1, Archbishop Kiprianós Square*

Hadjigeorgákis Kornésios House   (U/E5)

Awarded the Europa Nostra Prize in 1988, this museum shows the lifestyle of a rich Greek in 18th-century Cyprus.

The building housing it was probably a Venetian palace and this is where Hadjigeorgákis Kornésios and his family lived from 1779 to 1809. During that time he held the office of Dragoman, which meant that he was the island's highest Christian official at the time. The Dragoman oversaw tax collection in the interest of both the Christian Church and the Turkish sultanate. He was also the spokesman for the Christian community and, in this capacity, always had direct access to the Sultan.

The interior of this beautifully restored house shows how Oriental taste prevailed in Cyprus during Turkish rule. *Mon – Fri 8 am – 2 pm, Sat 9 am – 1 pm, admission 75¢, Patriarch Gregórios Street*

Icon Museum (U/E4)

★ Housed in a wing of the new Archbishop's Palace, the Icon Museum's collection includes well over 100 of the finest and most precious Cypriot icons and mosaics. The works exhibited here date from the 8th to the 18th century and represent a survey of styles, some of them revealing Western influence, and the subject matter of Byzantine art. *Mon – Fri 9 am – 4.30 pm, Sat 9 am – 1 pm, admission CYP 1, Archbishop Kiprianós Square*

Levéndis Museum (U/C5)

This museum at the edge of Laikí Gitoniá houses a representative collection of documents and objects that convey interesting insights into life in Nicosía over the past three centuries. *Tues – Sun 10 am – 4.30 pm, admission free, Hippócrates Street*

Museum of the National Struggle (U/E4)

The haunting exhibits in this museum bear tragic witness to the struggle of the EOKA against British colonial rule. Newspaper clippings and photos, letters and the pathetic personal belongings of freedom fighters who were hanged, a reconstruction of a gallows chamber and weapons recall the events of 1955–60. *Mon – Fri 8 am – 2.30 pm and 3 pm – 5.30 pm, admission 25¢, Archbishop Kiprianós Square*

State Collection of Contemporary Art (U/D6)

Permanent exhibition of painting and sculpture by Cypriot artists from 1930 to the present. *Mon – Fri 10 am – 5 pm, Sat 10 am – 1 pm, admission 25¢, Stassinós Avenue/Krítis Street*

Cyprus Museum (U/A–B5)

★ The most magnificent and important finds made by archaeologists on Cyprus are exhibited in the 16 rooms of this conveniently small and well ordered museum, built by the British in the early 20th century. Two hours spent here will leave you with insight into the island's cultural development from the Late Neolithic to the early Middle Ages.

Room 1 shows that people who lived nearly 8,000 years ago had the same basic needs as we have today. Cruciform idols made of andesite stone were probably worn as amulets to ward off supernatural evils. Necklaces like the ones here made of tubular shells and cornelian, on the other hand, were worn as jewellery. Stone bowls as well as clay dishes and jugs were made for domestic use. This 6,000-year-old pottery is early evidence that man was not merely trying to make functional objects for everyday living; the vessels were also intended to be beautiful. Some basins and jugs were painted red; others have highly polished surfaces and are often decorated with wavy lines incised in the slick while it was still wet with a toothed, comb-like implement. This early type of pottery is known to archaeologists as combed ware.

Room 2 affords glimpses into early Bronze Age life. Three fine terracotta figurative models represent peasants ploughing and temple scenes. The glossy, red pottery vessels are not conventionalized, as if their makers were still trying to settle on a style. Some of these vessels are large: up to seven gourd-shaped individual vessels are united to form a composite whole. The rims of others are imaginatively decorated with representations of animal and human heads.

Room 3 takes you on a 'quick tour' through the later history of ancient Cypriot pottery. Here there are vessels imported from Athens, Crete and Mycenae, which is where the famous Zeus Crater came from. On it is a representation of the father of the gods with the scales of fate determining the destiny of warriors going into battle. Two 7th-century BC vessels are magnificent exemplars of the free-field style. One of them boasts a depiction of a bull sniffing a lotus blossom; the other has a styl-

ized bird like a crane or heron holding a fish in its long thin bill.

Room 4 contains some of originally 2,000 terracotta votive statues and figurines found in an Archaic sanctuary on the north coast. They are displayed just as the archaeologists found them in the earth. The smallest votive figurines are only 10 cm high, but some of the largest statues are nearly life-size. The features of some are so highly individualized that they may even represent portraits of the votaries who expected the deity to protect them from harm.

Rooms 5 and 6 deal with the development of large sculpture on Cyprus. The earliest pieces still reveal strong Oriental influence. Later the spirit of the Roman Empire prevails. A particularly impressive exhibit is an over 2-metre-high bronze statue of the Roman Emperor Septimius Severus.

Room 7 deals with two fields of archaeology. The front half is distinctive for a wide variety of objects associated with the island's main source of revenue in antiquity: copper. There are copper ingots from the Bronze Age in the form of ox-hides, copper scales and copper artefacts such as meat skewers and cult statues: the celebrated Horned God from Énkomi and a second figure, which may be a deity, who is standing on an ox-hide ingot, brandishing a spear.

At the back of Room 7 hangs a Roman mosaic with a representation of Leda and the swan. The display cases contain Roman glass, ancient coins, jewellery and Byzantine silver plates. Two outstanding pieces are a

Late Bronze Age silver bowl inlaid with a continuous frieze of bulls' heads alternating with lotus blossoms in gold and niello and a sceptre dating from the 11th century BC surmounted by a cloisonné sphere on which stand two cloisonné hawks.

Room 8 contains reconstructions, replete with skeletons, tracing the development of burial customs on Cyprus from the Late Neolithic to the 5th century BC.

Room 9 is reserved for grave stelae (6th–3rd centuries BC).

Room 10 gives an overview of the ancient Cypriot scripts.

Room 11 is the repository of finds from the Royal Tombs at Salamís. Notable exhibits are ivory work from royal furnishings and a huge bronze cauldron on an iron tripod dating from the early 8th century BC. A side room is highly instructive on methods of copper smelting and working.

Room 12 deals with more tombs and caves.

Room 13 is full of Roman statues, which were brought from ancient Salamís.

Room 14 again recalls prehistoric Cyprus with a wealth of fascinating small artefacts. There are models of chariots, which may have been children's toys, and terracotta figures of women in childbirth as well as flat idols dating from the Early Bronze Age. *Mon–Sat 9 am–5 pm, Sun 10 am–1 pm, admission CYP 1.50, 1 Museum Street*

RESTAURANTS

Most restaurants in the old town are located in *Laikí Gitoniá* or close by. In the new part of the city restaurants are few and far between, although there are some old tavernas here too, near the intersection of *Evágoras* and *Makários Avenues.*

Acropolis (U/B5)
◉ Old-style taverna near the old town; good *mezé*, wine from the barrel. *Daily except Sun 12 noon–3 pm and 7 pm–midnight, 12 Leónidas Street, category 2*

Archontico (U/C5)
Attractively appointed taverna, popular amongst tourists and locals alike, serving good *mezé. Daily 12 noon–3 pm and 7 pm–midnight, Laikí Gitoniá, category 1*

Mattheos (U/D4)
Unpretentious family-run taverna with a large selection of hot food, near Faneroméni Church. *Daily except Sun 10 am–6 pm, Léfkonos Street, category 3*

Xefoto (U/C5)
★ Cypriots flock to this taverna in the evenings. Andreas, the proprietor, speaks English and serves excellent *mezé* and wine from the barrel; guests, and often the proprietor too, sing and dance to live Greek music (from 9.30 pm). *Daily from 11 am, Laikí Gitoniá, category 2*

SHOPPING

The main shopping streets are *Lédra* and *Onásgoras Streets* in the old town and *Makários Avenue* in the new part of the city. Most souvenir shops are in *Laikí Gitoniá.*

MAM (U/C5)
Specialist bookseller for aficionados of literature on Cyprus, Cy-

priot folk music and postcards with historical subject matter. *Laikí Gitoniá*

Markets

❧ More interesting than the old-town market hall (**U/D4,** *Platía Dimarchías, 7.30 am – 1 pm*) are the *Wednesday market on the Constanza Bastion* (**U/D5 - 6,** *7 am – 5 pm*) and the market in the new city (**U/F6,** *Evgenias & Antoníou Theodótou Avenue, Mon – Sat 7.30 am – 1 pm, Mon – Fri 4 pm – 6.30 pm; in winter 8 am – 5 pm*).

State Handicrafts Centre   (O)

All the crafts practised on the island with wares for sale at fixed prices. *Mon – Fri 7.30 am – 2.30 pm, Sept– May also Thurs 3 pm – 6 pm, 186 Athalassía Street (not far from where the Lárnaka-Límassol motorway starts)*

HOTELS

Classic   (U/B4)

Modern hotel with tastefully decorated interior and cosy atmosphere right on the city wall near the Páfos Gate. *57 rooms, 94 Regaena Street, Tel. 02 / 46 40 06, Fax 36 00 72, category 2*

Holiday Inn   (U/B5)

Fabulous comfort, in the old town right at the city wall. Indoor swimming pool and workout room, non-smokers' floors. *140 rooms, 70 Regaena Street, Tel. 02 / 47 51 31, Fax 47 33 37, category 1*

Rimi   (U/C5)

☥ Centrally located in the old town right at Laikí Gitoniá. *26 rooms, 5 Sólonos Street, Tel. 02/463153, category 3*

ENTERTAINMENT

Aegeon   (U/F3)

❧ Taverna with lots of atmosphere, near Famagústa Gate; excellent *mezé*, superb service. *Daily from 7 pm, 38 Hector Street, category 1*

Bastione   (U/F4)

☥ Stylish bar in an old house right at the Famagústa Gate. Venue for yuppies of all nationalities with international music. *Daily from 8 pm, 3 Athinás Avenue*

Cellari   (U/E4)

❧ A great place for Greek music in the old town; almost touristless. Dancing at times. *Daily from 9.45 pm, 25 Korais Street*

INFORMATION

Cyprus
Tourism Organization   (U/C5)

Laikí Gitoniá, Tel. 44 42 64

In the spirit of Marco Polo

Marco Polo was the first true world traveller. He travelled with peaceful intentions forging links between the East and the West. His aim was to discover the world, and explore different cultures and environments without changing or disrupting them. He is an excellent role model for the travellers of today and the future. Wherever we travel we should show respect for other peoples and the natural world.

WWF

Asínou (104/A3)

★ Medieval monks loved solitude. That is why they settled at the upper end of a valley on the fringes of the Tróodos, remote from all villages in a setting of woods and pastures. All that is left of the Panagía Forviótissa Monastery, which they built in Asínou District, is its church. The living quarters and offices, built of wood and daub, have vanished. This church is one of the greatest treasures of Cypriot art.

From the outside the little, single-aisled church, with the eaves of its tiled roof reaching nearly to the ground, looks more like a granary than a house of worship. However, closer scrutiny reveals a second, older barrel vault in the nave and domes above the narthex in front. The tiled roof, probably inspired by Crusader architecture, was simply clapped on and pulled down as low as possible to protect the church from wind and weather. This explains why the frescoes in this church are in such a superb state of preservation. The earliest date from 1105/6 and glow with all the vibrancy of 900 years ago, thanks to thorough cleaning 25 years ago, which restored the brilliant colour to nearly pristine condition.

One of the most interesting of the nave frescoes is above the small north door. On the right is a small-scale portrait of the donor's wife. Standing in front of her, the donor himself is portrayed on a larger scale as he symbolically hands a model of the church to the Virgin, who in turn is depicted on yet a larger scale. Christ, the recipient of the church, is enthroned facing her. Behind him are angels in splendid robes.

Just as fascinating is a representation of the Forty Martyrs of Sebaste in the left-hand corner of the church. Almost naked, freezing, exhausted and bleeding copiously from wounds, 39 of these soldiers, who were persecuted by the governor of Sebaste, are depicted on the ice of a frozen lake. The fortieth, however, has succumbed to the delights of a warm bath on the shore, his reward for repudiating Christianity. A volunteer emerges from the other side of the intrados to take his place amongst the martyrs. Above the martyrs float 40 crowns sent down to them by Christ.

The narthex, also completely covered with frescoes, was added in the 14th century. Next to the door between it and the church is a revealing hunting scene with two hunting dogs on leads and two Cypriot moufflons in the mountains. The scenes of the entry into Paradise on the left-hand side wall as well as several donor portraits in panels are also beautifully rendered. *The priest at Nikitári, the village before Asínou, keeps the key to the church. You'll probably find him in the church or otherwise in the village. Donations usual, 31 km from Nicosía*

Fikárdou (104/C5)

The little village near Machairás Monastery has been a protected historic monument since 1978. Only a dozen or so people still live here. Public funds have paid for the restoration of many of the houses as they were in the 18th and 19th centuries so that Fikárdou today is really an open-air theme park or museum village. The houses, built of rubble masonry and clay, are two-storeyed. Two of the oldest, dating from the 16th century, are now ethnographic museums in which old furniture and household utensils as well as photos documenting village life and the restoration work are displayed. *Museums May – Sept Tues – Fri 9.30 am – 4.30 pm, Sat 9.30 am – 4 pm, Sun 10 am – 1.30 pm, Oct – Apr Tues – Fri 9 am – 6 pm, Sat 9.30 am – 5 pm, Sun 9.30 am – 3.30 pm, admission 75c, 40 km from Nicosía*

Ágios Iraklídios Convent   (105/D4)

Like the royal tombs at Tamassós, the convent is at the edge of the Mesaoría near the little village of Politikó, which is becoming deserted. You pass through the village to find the walls of the convent rising above a lovely olive grove, a charming motif for photographers. Since 1962 the nuns have been living here in a Garden of Eden they have created themselves. Visitors tend to find the cloister quadrangle, which is like a garden, more interesting than the building. Swallows nest in the cloister arcades and the nuns sell printed icons and marzipan of their own making (not chocolate covered as it is in Europe) in the convent shop.

St Iraklídios, to whom the convent is consecrated, was anointed the first bishop of Tamassós, a copper-producing centre from the 8th century BC, by the Apostle Paul. Iraklídios was martyred in the mid-1st century, when Christianity was basically still an underground sect. His skull is venerated as a relic in the convent church.

The church is a four-part structure. In front of it is a transverse vestibule with an open arcade, an exonarthex. On the right it leads to a cross-domed church, built in the 14th century over a grotto, which is said to be the saint's grave. You can climb down into the grotto through a trapdoor or more easily from behind the east side of the church.

The present convent church is two-aisled and dates from the 15th/16th centuries. You can still pick out traces of the earlier frescoes and parts of a floor mosaic, which belonged to an Early Christian basilica dating from 400, when Christianity became the Cypriot state religion. Parts of the mosaic have been preserved on the right next to the cross-domed church. On the far left in the iconstasis of the convent church is a notable icon of a Cypriot type depicting the Virgin suckling the infant Christ. *Open during the day (closed 12 noon – 3 pm), admission free, 21 km from Nicosía*

Ágios Panteleímon Convent   (104/C3)

This convent is in a peaceful location at the southern edge of the Mesaoría in the pretty small village of Mitseró. Built in the 18th century, it declined in the late 19th century, but was restored in the 1960s. The cloister garden is lovely. *Open during the day, admission free, 29 km from Nicosía*

Machairás Monastery (Makherás) (104/C5)

A tortuous narrow paved road winds up from the Mesaoría through dense forests to an elevation of nearly 900 m on the slopes of Mount Kiónia. You can walk back down the river valley from the top in about 4 hours to Politikó, the site of ancient Tamassós. At the head of the valley and with superb views down on it is the monastery of 'Our Lady of the Knife', Panagía Makherás. There has been a monastery here since the 12th century but all the present buildings and the rather plain church in the narrow court was not built until after the last fire at the monastery, which was in 1892. The church interior is decorated with frescoes in the Byzantine style. The monks here are not very welcoming to non-Orthodox visitors because all too many tourists have arrived at the monastery noisy and inappropriately dressed. Groups no longer gain entry but individual tourists may be admitted. *Mon, Tues and Thurs 9 am – 12 noon, admission free, 32 km from Nicosía*

Mitseró (104/B-C3)

This village at the northern edge of the Mesaoría near Ágios Panteleímon Convent was a copper-mining centre until 1979. Slag-heaps left over from ancient copper-smelting still abound in the area; many of them are startlingly black and menacing. *30 km from Nicosía*

North Nicosía (105/F1)

If the only checkpoint where foreign visitors may cross the Green Line has not been closed yet again by the Greek Cypriots for political reasons, you can undertake an excursion to the occupied part of the old town of Nicosía without too much hassle. In just half a day you'll be able to find out a lot more about old Nicosía.

From the checkpoint at the old Ledra Palace Hotel, it takes about 10 minutes via the main road to reach the Kerínia Gate, the most important modern break in the medieval city wall in the northern part of Nicosía. If you continue down the main road into the old town, the first thing you'll see on your left is what was once an establishment of whirling dervishes and is now a museum for Turkish Cypriot folk art.

Next comes Ataturk Square, which has heavy traffic today. In 1570 the Venetians erected an ancient granite column from Salamís here. Near it is a modern hotel, the Saray, which has a rooftop bar and a restaurant open all day. From here you have a good view of the whole of Nicosía and begin to grasp the implications of the madness that has severed the city and the republic.

Three buildings in the heart of the old town in north Nicosía are noteworthy: the ★ *Selimiye Mosque*, built early in the 13th century as a Gothic church for Crusaders; the former greater caravanserai, in Turkish *Büyük Han*, and the lesser caravanserai, *Kumarcilar Han* which is now a museum.

Everything you might want to visit is open in the morning. The currency used in north Nicosía is the Turkish lira. Banks here will even change CYP, Cypriot líres.

Peristeróna (104/B2)

❖ If you like to take pictures, this large village off the main road from Nicosía into the Tróodos Mountains is well

The churches of Saints Barnabas and Hilarion in Peristeróna

worth a short trip. A mosque and a church with impressive domes some 1,000 years old stand peaceably next to each other on the bank of a riverbed that is nearly always dry. The *kafeníon* in the square where the church is might be just the place for you to observe Cypriot village life at leisure. *Mosque closed; the key to church is in the kafeníon. 27 km from Nicosía*

Tamassós (105/D4)

Before you enter the little village of Politikó (Ágios Iraklídios Convent is on the outskirts of town), you will see a sign pointing to the Royal Tombs at Tamassós. Renowned for its copper since the 8th century BC, most of the city has yet to be ex-

cavated. Only the foundation walls of an Aphrodite-Astarte temple and some ancient workshops have been dug up at the car park in front of the Royal Tombs.

Two stone tombs dating from the 6th century BC are particularly noteworthy because they are skeuomorphs; that is, they were made in imitation of other materials and structures in wood, stone and terracotta, in this case dwellings for living people. Steps lead down into the tombs and they are covered with massive limestone slabs. The ceiling beams, doorframes, false doors and windows, window balusters and beam-end bosses at the entrance suggest Egyptian and Near Eastern influence. Even the capitals at the entrance to the tomb chambers are proof that, in some remote places at least, Asia Minor shaped the prevailing taste in 6th-century Cyprus far more than Greece did. *Tues – Fri 9 am – 3 pm, Sat/Sun 10 am – 3 pm, take a torch with you, admission 75c, 20 km from Nicosía*

Vyzakiá (104/A3)

The village of Vyzakiá is on the Nicosía-Asínou road just before Nikitári. Shortly after leaving the village, if you drive on towards Asínou, you see the tiny church consecrated to the archangel with its shed-like roof and some remarkable 16th-century frescoes. They are vernacular in style, a pleasant change from the usual Byzantine formalism. *Ask for the key in the village kafeníon, donation usual, 25 km from Nicosía*

Paradise endangered

The untouched natural beauty of the west of the island is at risk from tourism

The west of the island is more sparsely populated than the rest of Cyprus. The region's biggest city, Páfos, has retained all the charm of a small town. Pólis, the second largest city, is hardly more than a village. Only tourism has challenged agriculture as the region's main source of revenue since the mid-1980s. In an era of environmental awareness, most hotels have been planned to fit into their natural setting.

In the west the island climate is milder and more temperate than elsewhere on Cyprus. Bananas can even be cultivated in plantations near Páfos. Peanuts and tobacco are major crops and all sorts of fruit are grown here. There are at least as many carob as olive groves dotting the mountain slopes along the coast. Wine is grown in the mountains.

There is no manufacturing to speak of. Nature still reigns supreme. Páfos District boasts the densest and most extensive forests on the island, including the

Fishermen at work in Páfos harbour

cedar forests in the beautiful Valley of the Cedars. Although British military exercises still go on here, the Ákamas Peninsula in the far west is virtually uninhabited. Sea turtles go ashore here to lay their eggs. Marvellous footpaths criss-cross this untouched country.

Yet this paradise, too, is endangered. Since hotels have been spreading out along the coast north-west of Páfos, the once deserted beaches where the turtles lay their eggs are now frequented by growing numbers of thoughtless holidaymakers. The inhabitants of the villages fringing the peninsula are just as eager to make money as the farmers at Agía Nápa, Lárnaka and Límassol ever were with the advent of mass tourism.

Páfos District is steeped in history. After all, in antiquity Páfos was an important city-kingdom with a major Aphrodite sanctuary thronged by votaries from the entire Greek-speaking world. In the Ptolemaic and Roman eras the provincial governors sent to Cyprus from Rome and Egypt ruled the island from Páfos.

MARCO POLO SELECTION: PÁFOS

1 Old harbour
Fresh fish all year round
(page 65)

2 House of Dionysus
Ancient mosaics that
recount myths (page 66)

**3 Ethnographic Museum
Geroskípou** You'll see how
silk is made (page 71)

4 Páno Panagiá
Historic mountain village
(page 73)

5 Ágios Neófytos Monastery
800-year-old portraits of
a hermit (page 71)

6 Pólis
A resort with a split per-
sonality (page 73)

PÁFOS

(110/A–B2-3) History has shaped Páfos (pop. 35,000) as a distinctive cultural landscape. Tavernas and hotels rub shoulders with ancient and medieval buildings throughout the modern city. The most attractive tavernas, the ones down along the fishing port, serve guests on the very spot where worshippers of Aphrodite landed 2,000 years ago and ships were laden with fragrant wood from the vast cedar forests as well as copper and other Cypriot natural resources.

Páfos is divided into three distinct sections. First there's Káto Páfos on the sea. Its fishing port underwent dredging and reconstruction in 1993. To the north and east of it stretches the sprawling hotel section, with a sprinkling of local residents, gardens and undeveloped property. The string of hotels has crept along the beach as far as the community of Geroskípou.

Most of the city's inhabitants live in the upper part of town at Ktíma, which was built in the Turkish period on a plateau 2 – 3 km inland. Shops and small businesses catering for residents' daily needs, schools and official buildings dominate the townscape. Souvenir shops, tavernas and bars dot the coast.

Finally, the site of the ancient city of Páfos, is known as Palaiá (Old) Páfos. It was abandoned as early as 321 BC for Néa Páfos, which was situated where modern Ktíma and Káto Páfos have grown up. The still rural village of Koúklia and expanses of ancient ruins and rubble cover the site of what was ancient Palaiá Páfos.

The city's history began at Palaiá Páfos. By the 4th century BC, it was presumably no longer economically expedient to be situated so far from the sea. King Níkokles decided to build a new city close by but right on the sea. Most of the inhabitants of Palaiá Páfos moved in 321 BC to the new city. Not long afterwards the Egyptian Ptolemies took over the island and made Néa Páfos the seat of the island administration. The city was also capital of Cyprus when in 58 BC the country was made a province of the Roman Empire. The island was governed by a proconsul who resided near the port in a large villa decorated with beautiful mosaic floors. To judge by the number of grand basilicas there, Néa Páfos seems to have sustained a large population on into the Early Christian era. During the Middle Ages Páfos dwindled into a provincial backwater, which in some ways it has remained to this day despite the inroads of tourism.

SIGHTS

Agía Solomoní
Pagan tombs hewn into the rock were still being put to various uses in the Christian era: as quarries, as prison cells or even as Christian chapels. The ancient tomb of St Salomoní was turned into a chapel. An odd tree, with handkerchiefs and scraps of cloth tied to its branches, stands at the head of the stair leading down into the chapel. This ancient practice, not confined to Cyprus, is supposed by supplicants to enhance the efficacy of prayer. *Apóstolos Pávlos Avenue, admission free*

Harbour
★ The harbour breakwater, now used only by fishermen and excursion boats, was built on the foundations of one of two ancient moles. Some of the ancient blocks of stone are visible at the end of the modern breakwater. A Turkish fort at the head of the breakwater affords a fine view of Páfos and is certainly worth visiting for this alone. *Fort: May – Sept daily 10 am – 6 pm, Oct – April Mon – Fri 7.30 am – 2.30 pm, Thurs also 3 pm – 6 pm, Sat and Sun 9 am – 5 pm, admission 75c*

Tombs of the Kings
No ancient houses have been preserved in Páfos. However, tombs dating from the two centuries of Ptolemaic rule before the Romans annexed Cyprus give a vivid picture of domestic architecture in that highly prosperous era. The finest of these tombs were hewn out of the bedrock close to the sea. They boast inner courts surrounded by columns and pillars from which the tomb chambers may be entered. The necropolis is, in fact, like an underground city. In one of the courts, a massive free-standing block of stone conceals an inner stair leading down to a well. Other parts of the rock were used for tomb chambers. These sumptuous sepulchres, once believed – erroneously – by ar-

---

Names can be confusing

Káto Páfos: The seaside section of Páfos.
Néa Páfos: All of modern Páfos, including Ktíma, the upper town.
Palaiá Páfos (pronounced: Paleá Páfos): Ancient pre-Ptolemaic Páfos near the modern village of Koúklia.
Páfos: The whole city.

---

chaeologists to have contained royal burials, are not the only ones here. The bedrock is honeycombed with more modest tomb chambers. Although kings were not buried in the necropolis, it was probably used by the Ptolemaic governors of the island and their families. *May – Oct daily 8 am – 7.30 pm, Nov – Apr Mon – Fri 8 am – 5 pm, Sat and Sun 9 am – 5 pm, admission 75c, Tombs of the Kings Road*

Mosaics

The centre of the Roman city was situated to the north-west of the modern fishing port. It was surrounded by high walls, but they have not been preserved. Several spacious villas and administration buildings decorated with magnificent mosaic floors stood here. Since their rediscovery in 1962, they have been uncovered like leaves of a glowing picture book of Greek mythology and so painstakingly restored that a visit here could be the high point of your Cyprus holiday.

Most of these mosaics date from the 3rd and 4th centuries AD. The consummate artistry with which they were executed, the number of mosaics extant and their excellent state of preservation have made them a UNESCO World Cultural Heritage site. Four houses have mosaic floors and they have been named by archaeologists after the subject matter of the mosaic representations in them. The sites are very close together, and one ticket enables to visit all four.

★ The large mosaic depicting a grape-harvest scene in the *House of Dionysus* is particularly noteworthy. It is enlivened by a wealth of quirky details: a rabbit nibbles green leaves, a partridge pecks at grapes and a snake with flickering tongue slithers up to the delectable fruit. A field hand carries a basket brimful of grapes in his right hand, while managing to balance a second on his left shoulder. Another field hand is depicted cutting grapes. You'll have no trouble spotting the overseer because this figure is noticeably better dressed and holds a stick in his hand.

Another mosaic is also closely associated with wine. The elderly Athenian farmer Icarius is depicted holding the reigns of a yoke of oxen in his left hand. The two animals draw a two-wheeled cart on which wine is being transported in goatskins. This is the first wine transport in history, for Icarius was the first person to have been initiated by the god Dionysus into the mysteries of viticulture and wine-making. The god's lessons were to have lethal consequences for Icarius, however. In the right-hand lower corner two intoxicated boys are represented. Mythology has it that they forced the king to let them taste his wine and indulged in so much of it that they fell into a drunken stupor. What is not shown here is that friends found them in that state and murdered Icarius, assuming that he had poisoned the youths. The god Dionysus takes this in his stride: he is shown flirting with lovely Akmi on the left in the mosaic.

In all the other mosaics ancient mythology has been rendered with similar grace and exuberance. The best way to familiarize yourself with the mosaics is to go on a guided tour of them before returning to them with a guidebook in English bought at the ticket window.

From the House of Dionysus, you proceed to the House of Aion, where five panels contain further representations of mythological subject matter. Then you go on to the House of Theseus, which boasts an extraordinary mosaic with a large round panel at its centre. The Athenian hero Theseus is depicted at the centre after conquering the Minotaur in the form of a wild bull in the Cretan Labyrinth. The Labyrinth is allegorically personified on the left below Theseus. The Minotaur, showing signs of wear, is below the hero on the right. At the top right, the island of Crete is personified as a king. At the top left is a representation of the Cretan king's daughter, Ariadne, whose ball of thread enabled Theseus to find his way out of the Labyrinth.

From the House of Theseus, you come to the House of Orpheus, which has three more fine mosaics. *May – Sept daily 8 am – 7.30 pm, Oct – Apr Mon – Fri 8 am – 5 pm, Sat and Sun 9 am – 5 pm, admission CYP 1.50, above the fishing port*

Odeon

〰️ Close to the houses with the mosaic floors, a little white lighthouse rises into the almost invariably blue sky. Below this relic of British rule, archaeologists have excavated the Roman odeon, a small theatre used by the Romans for lyric poetry contests and musical performances. Even now the odeon is occasionally used for concerts, folklore events and plays put on by amateur groups. From any of the 12 tiers of seats, you gaze out across a large open space, which in antiquity was thronged with people, the bustling forum or marketplace. *Above the fishing port*

St Paul's Column

It is related of the Apostle Paul that he was in Páfos to demonstrate the power of Christianity to the Roman proconsul or governor, which he did by striking blind the pagan sorcerer Elymas, who was active at the governor's court. Furthermore, local legend has it that Paul was flogged publicly in Páfos. The flagellation column to which he was tied while being beaten is still shown to visitors. It stands in what were the precincts of an Early Christian basilica abutting the medieval Panagía Chryssopolítissa church.

Saránda Kolónnes

〰️ One of the most poorly preserved yet most beautiful castle ruins in Cyprus can be found just above the fishing port. Built by Crusaders shortly after they conquered the island in 1192, it was destroyed by an earthquake only 30 years later. From then on it was quarried for stone. Its name, meaning '40 columns' refers to the fact that 40 granite columns from the Roman forum were incorporated into it. Roman columns support the walls of the castle entrance in the east and were used as thresholds as well as barriers to mangers in the stalls where the knights stabled their horses. *Above the fishing port*

MUSEUMS

District Museum (archaeological)
This little museum exhibits superb gold jewellery dating from the 15th century BC to the 3rd century AD, fine pieces of Roman glass and, rather unexpectedly, a number of Roman clay hot-water bottles shaped like parts of the male human body. Perhaps they were made for particular dignitaries or they may have belonged to a physician who used them homeopathically to treat patients suffering from rheumatism. *Mon–Fri 8 am – 5 pm (Thurs 3 pm – 6 pm), Sat and Sun 10 am – 1 pm, admission 75c, Digenís Street*

Byzantine Museum
A clearly ordered collection of icons dating from the 12th to the 18th centuries is presented here, as well as liturgical vestments and vessels. *Mon–Fri 9 am – 5 pm (June–Sept until 7 pm), Sat 9 am – 2 pm, admission CYP 1, Andréa Ioánnou Street, Ktíma*

Ethnographic Museum
A villa built in 1894 houses this private museum, which exhibits obviously functional yet distinctively decorative artefacts and utensils used in Cypriot daily life over the past few centuries. *Mon – Sat 9 am – 1 pm, Mon – Fri also 2 pm – 5 pm (May–Sept 3 pm – 7 pm), Sun 10 am – 1 pm, admission 50c, 1 Exó Vríssi Street*

RESTAURANTS

Pelican
The pick of the tavernas serving delicious seafood on the port, with tables inside and outside. Its mascot is a live pelican, which certainly enjoys having its picture taken. *Daily from 11 am, category 1*

Thomas Jungle Pub-Restaurant
Modern, reasonably priced restaurant serving Cypriot and international cuisine; lots of salads; a huge selection of cocktails. The proprietor speaks German and English. *Daily from 9 am, Tombs of the Kings Road, category 3*

SHOPPING

Market hall
The market hall in Ktíma is much too small to accommodate all the farmers who want to sell their produce, especially on Saturday morning, so a bustling and entertaining weekly open-air market has grown up around it. *Agorás Street*

State Handicrafts Centre
All the souvenirs worth seeing can be found here. *Apostle Paul Avenue*

HOTELS

Annabelle
A first-class hotel situated next to the beach, only a short walk away from the fishing port. A small sandy beach replenished each year, 2 pools. *198 rooms, Posidónos Street, Tel. 06 / 23 83 33, Fax 24 55 02, category 1*

Kiniras

An unpretentious old-town hotel with 18 rooms. *91 Archiepiskopos Makários Avenue, Tel. 06 / 24 16 04, Fax 24 21 76, category 3*

Within the city limits there are only a few small, artificially created sandy beaches in front of the hotels. The big beaches start at Geroskípou and below the old British lighthouse at the Roman odeon. To the west of Páfos stretch superb wide sand and pebble beaches easily reached by public bus lines.

Water sports are offered by the large hotels, which also feature diving courses and excursions. The oldest golf course on Cyprus (18 holes, 72 par for the course, 5,687 m for men, 5,222 m for ladies) is 10 km out of town and south-east of the village of Tsáda. The green fee is about CYP 32 on weekdays and CYP 36 at weekends.

Demókritos

A large taverna with a folklore floor show and excellent *mezé*, in the hotel section. *Daily from 8 pm, Ágios Antónios Street*

Thessalonika

Typical live *bouzoúki* performances (expensive) in the cellar. *Wed – Mon midnight – 6 am, Ikárou Street, Káto Páfos*

Cyprus Tourism Organization

In the airport building, open during all arrivals, Tel. 06 / 42 28 33, and 3 Gladstone Street, Ktíma, Tel. 06 / 23 28 41

Ágios Geórgios   (100/A6)

The westernmost village on the south coast of Cyprus is situated above the sea in the midst of gardens and fields. If you hire a car for your stay in order to reach the beaches in the surrounding area, you can save money by booking a room in a private house or one at the little Yeronissos Hotel, which is quiet and off the beaten track.

In any case Ágios Geórgios is well worth at least a day trip because there are three Early Christian basilicas in idyllic settings close by. Some walls are still over 1 m high; mosaic floors are notable for geometric designs and crosses with representations of animals, birds and tortoises. *Always accessible, admission free, 20 km from Páfos; accommodation: Yeronissos Hotel, Tel. 06 / 62 10 78, category 3*

Aphrodite's Bath
(Loutrá tis Aphrodítis)   (100/B3)

At the end of a short paved path leading through a lush river valley, you suddenly come upon a small pond fed by a spring bubbling up in a grotto framed by a fig tree. Ferns and flowers fringe its rocky banks. Legend has it that this idyllic spot was the bathing pool most favoured by the goddess Aphrodite. One day she was seen here by the Athenian prince Acamas. Dalliance which grew into a passionate love affair between the immortal beauty and the handsome prince aroused the ire of Zeus, father of the gods. He ordered the goddess of love to abstain from infatuation for mere mortals and banished her to Mount Olympus, the dwelling place of the gods in Greece. *Always accessible, admission free, 40 km from Páfos*

Coral Bay (110/A1)

A wide and shallow bay with a sandy beach, which gave its name to a new, rapidly growing development of holiday flats, houses and shops. By now the development has spilled over into neighbouring Corallia Bay, which has mainly pebble beaches. A narrow neck of land separates the two coves. On it archaeologists have excavated what is left of a Late Bronze Age settlement. The fortification wall surrounding it is 3,500 years old and well enough preserved to be easily recognizable, even from quite a distance. *Mon – Sat 10 am – 4 pm, admission 75c, 13 km from Páfos*

Droúseia (Droúsha) (100/B5)

❂ This mountain village is the perfect spot for holidaymakers who are looking for peace and quiet. Here they can spend a few days and do some good walking. Former villagers who are now living abroad have built a modern hotel replete with a pool and panoramic views, the *Droshia*

Heights (46 rooms, Tel.06 / 33 23 51, Fax 33 23 53, category 2). 37 km from Páfos

Émba (110/B2)

The village *kafeníons* are still unspoilt. At the centre of the settlement is a remarkable 12th-century church consecrated to Our Lady of Golden Charity, Panagía Chryseleoússa. *4 km from Páfos*

Rocks of Aphrodite (111/D4–5)

❂❂ Several deserted pebble beaches are set against a long backdrop of cliffs tapering off at the western end to a small beach. Here several rocks rise out of the sea. Called 'The Rocks of the Roman' (Pétra tou Roméou, which now means simply 'of the Greek'), they are advertized internationally by tourist agencies as the Rocks of Aphrodite with the enticing claim that the Goddess Aphrodite rose from the sea foam on this very spot. *22 km from Páfos*

Geroskípou (110/B3)

The name of this village means 'of the Sacred Grove', indicating that a grove consecrated to Aphrodite stood here in antiquity. Votaries seeking the favour of the goddess passed through it on their way from the harbour of Néa Páfos to the Aphrodite sanctuary at Palaiá Páfos. A popular local speciality is sold in the

---

Pygmalion and Aphrodite

In Greek mythology Pygmalion was an early king of Páfos. An enthusiastic amateur sculptor, he so adored the goddess Aphrodite that he made a statue of her. He implored the goddess to breathe life into the statue and, lo and behold: the marble lady came to life and he married her as Galatea, 'white as milk'.

village high street: *loukoúmia*. Known in English as Turkish Delight, *loukoúmia* are tough, chewy squares of fruit jelly dredged in icing sugar and eaten as a sweet in Near Eastern countries and in Greece. In September and October the side-streets look as if they were covered with thick greenish-brown carpets: peanuts laid out to dry. The recently smartened up *platía* at the centre of town is very lively. This is where the town's main attraction stands: the ancient church of Agía Paraskeví. So simple and rustic are its domes that it is thought to have been built in the 9th or 10th century. Some of the frescoes in it are non-representational, stylized plant motifs and crosses, suggesting an early date, even before 850.

Near the church is a little ★ *Ethnographic Museum*, which is informative on the cultivation of silkworms and the making of silk at Geroskípou, a craft practised here until World War II. *Key to the church kept by the shoemaker in the square; donations please. Museum Mon – Fri 7.30 am – 2.30 pm, Sept – June Thurs also 3 pm – 6 pm, admission 75c, 3 km from Páfos*

Ágios Neófytos
Monastery (110/B1)

★ One of the most beautiful monasteries in Cyprus is situated on the slopes of Mount Chárta (613 m) at the end of a green valley. It is consecrated to a Cypriot saint who lived here as a hermit from 1159. His solitude was soon invaded by other pious men who lived in caves in a rock wall the saint himself

had begun to turn into cells. Today you can still see the little grotto chapel, Neófytos's first hermit's cell, and the tomb he made for himself. The saint had these caves decorated with frescoes, two of them portraying Neófytos himself. One shows him standing, flanked by angels; in the other he is depicted kneeling before the throne of Christ, which is flanked by the Virgin Mary and St John, who are standing. The present monastery buildings across from the caves go back to the 15th century. Saint Neófytos's skull is preserved as a holy relic in the monastery church, which is surrounded by a lovely courtyard. The frescoes on the vaulting of the left-hand aisle of the nave date from about 1500. *Apr – Sept daily 9 am – 1 pm and 2 pm – 6 pm, Oct – Mar daily 9 am – 4 pm, admission 50c, 8 km from Páfos*

Panagía Chrysorrogiátissa
Monastery (101/E6)

〰️ Founded in the 12th century, the monastery is high above a valley in the western outliers of the Tróodos near the village of Páno Panagiá. The forecourt is remarkable for a cluster of clay ovens. Right next to the entrance is the monastery taverna. You can sample the excellent monastery wines on its shady terrace. The abbot's brother is your host.

At the centre of the not very spacious quadrangle is a church consecrated to the Virgin. It is famous for a miraculous icon of the Virgin, which is said to have been painted by St Luke the Evangelist. A small shop where wine is sold and workshops for restoring old icons open on to

Fishing boats in the lovely port of Lákki

the quadrangle. The monastery wine cellar is open to the public in the morning between September and spring. *Always open, admission free, 36 km from Páfos*

Koúklia (Palaiá Páfos) (111/D4)

West of Páfos is the most important ancient Aphrodite sanctuary on Cyprus. Situated on a flat plateau above the green coastal plain, it was sought out by votaries from the entire ancient world, especially in Roman times. At the sanctuary, worshippers took part in mysterious rites, which placed them under the protection of the goddess. All that is really known about them is that the Oriental practice of temple prostitution went on here too. Every Pafian woman had to sleep once with a stranger in the sanctuary before she could marry.

The ancient sanctuary, of which only very little is left, originally consisted of a closed court, the precinct in which the goddess was worshipped in the form of a large, dark stone. In the Roman era, a large perisytle court surrounded by columns was built at the entrance to the sanctuary. Remains of mosaics and the foundation walls can still be seen.

Right next to the excavation site is the Château de Covôcle, a fortified manor, which now houses a museum. In it is a stone that may have been a cult object in the ancient sanctuary. The manor itself is historic. The building as you see it today dates largely from the Turkish era. However, a spacious Gothic hall is an obvious reminder that the sugar-cane plantations of the Frankish kings of Cyprus were administered from here before the Venetian conquest.

May – Sept Mon – Fri 7.30 am – 6 pm, Sat and Sun 9 am – 5 pm, Oct – Apr Mon – Fri until 5 pm, Sat and Sun until 4 pm, admission 75c, 15 km from Páfos

Lákki (Látchi) (100/B3)

This little village, often said to boast the island's loveliest fishing port, is an interesting point of departure for beautiful excursions by boat along the Akamas Peninsula, which is dotted

72

with little beaches. We recommend the Porto Latchi Taverna for atmosphere *(daily 8 am – midnight, category 1)*, because it is in a restored, 300-year-old building which was a warehouse for carob beans. *36 km from Páfos*

Lémba (110/A2)

Painters, sculptors and potters work in Lémba. Near the road leading from Lémba to the sea, a Bronze Age settlement has been excavated. Next to it is a scholarly reconstruction of the over 4,500-year-old village. *Open to the public, admission free, 7 km from Páfos*

Páno Panagiá (101/F5)

★ A wine-growing vilage at an elevation of 800 m, this was the birthplace of Archbishop Makários. In the square where a monument to him stands, a small museum commemorates his life and work with photographs and documents. Here you can get the key to the humble house where he was born and spent the early years of his childhood. *Museum daily 9 am – 1 pmand 3 pm – 6 pm, admission 30c, 37 km from Páfos*

Pólis (100/C3)

★ ✝ Until the mid-1990s, Pólis was frequented by German backpackers. Now it is fast developing into a luxury resort. Holidaymakers who stay at the campsite in a eucalyptus grove or in small self-catering flats are still holding their own against those willing to spend CYP 116 and more a night for a suite in the luxurious Anassa Hotel *(185 rooms, Tel. 06 / 32 28 00, Fax 32 29 00)*. Travel agents and tour operators are geared to mountain biking and jeep tours for visitors who want adventure holidays; there is a riding stables and a wide range of water sports is offered. In 1999 an archaeological museum will open.

Stavrós tis Psókas (101/F4)

Lost in the forests of the western Tróodos there is a state forestry station. The *kafeníon* there is both a restaurant and a grocery store, which sells basic commodities. Just below it, anyone who has brought their own charcoal and meat can enjoy a real Cypriot barbecue with all the trimmings at tables and benches set up in a spacious, shady picnic area. There are some tame moufflons in an enclosure here if you haven't seen one yet. *44 km from Páfos*

Valley of the Cedars (Cedar Valley) (101/F4)

✝ In prehistoric times Cyprus was blanketed with cedar forests, although quite early on copper-smelting made inroads on them. In Greco-Roman antiquity, the forests were decimated to build ships and houses and to make charcoal for smelters and domestic use. In the 1930s the British colonial administration embarked on a reforestation programme on the wooded slopes of Mount Trípilos. Now over 30,000 cedars, most of them large examplars of their species, cover the area. The best view across the Valley of the Cedars is from the well marked footpath up Mount Trípilos (1,362 m), even if you only feel like a half-hour's walk. *52 km from Páfos (via Stavrós tis Psókas)*

Mountains and monasteries

The mountains round Ólympos, the island's highest peak, conceal art treasures in profusion

From far away it seems incredible that the loftiest peak in the Tróodos, Ólympos, is nearly 2,000 m high. When you see it from Nicosía or Límassol, you think you command a view of the entire massif. No wonder you'd swear Ólympos is at best half as high as it really is. The Tróodos is of only moderate elevation, with gently rounded peaks and few steep escarpments. This is hilly country with wooded slopes. Only when you drive or hike through it do you realize just how rugged the terrain is. Chain after chain of ridges recedes into the distance as if the mountains went on forever.

From many of the lower peaks you have sweeping panoramic views down to the sea or across the Mesaoría plain. Life goes on at a much slower pace in the mountain villages down below on the coast. In remote mountain fastnesses you come across inhabited monasteries and churches centuries old, many of them still adorned with medieval frescoes in a good state of preservation.

The Tróodos Mountains are well served with a network of paved roads and forest tracks, which are used for logging and fighting forest fires, should they break out. There are hotels in some villages; *kafeníons* and tavernas are everywhere. Round Mount Ólympos footpaths are well marked and nature trails initiate lovers of flowers and plants into the wonders of the island flora.

When planning a holiday in Cyprus, you might seriously consider staying in the mountains instead of down by the sea. If you have a hire car, you can pop down for a quick refreshing plunge in the sea and then return to the heavenly peace and quiet of the mountains.

The inhabitants of the Tróodos region do not depend on tourism as their main source of income. Those who don't commute daily to the coastal towns to work usually earn their livelihood in agriculture: wine-growing, orchards and raising sheep and goats. Until only a few years ago, mining, especially chrome and opencast asbestos

Pilgrims and patriots flock to Kýkko Monastery in the Tróodos

mining for global export, was the major industry in the Tróodos, but all operations in this sector have closed down.

SIGHTS

Agrós   (104/A5–6)
This large village (elevation 1,000 m) in the eastern Tróodos is in an idyllic setting amidst terraced vineyards. This is where the grapes for the sweet *commandaría* wine are grown. In April and May a distillery with its own pottery transforms the essences of commercially cultivated roses into rosewater. It is open to the public then.

Páno Amíandos   (103/E5)
Once a mining settlement, Páno Amíandos is set against the backdrop of an unsightly blot on the mountain scenery: a sprawling slag heap left over from the workings of the asbestos mine and bare, pocked slopes. Mining continued into the 1980s.

Galáta   (103/D4)
Galáta is in the Soléa Valley (elevation 600 m) on the north slope of the Tróodos, set amidst orchards and slender poplars. Even in the Middle Ages, the Byzantine nobility and after them afluent Venetians enjoyed coming here to escape the summer heat. Nowadays Galáta is eagerly sought out by Nicosía residents for cool evenings or weekends away from the sweltering capital. Fine 19th-century houses in the village include a beautifully restored caravanserai, called the *Haní Kalliana*, right on the road through town. Galáta also boasts four Byzantine churches with the shed-like roofs characteristic of the region. Two of them are certainly worth visiting for their lovely setting and their remarkable frescoes: Panagía Podíthou and Archangels. Ask at the large *kafeníon* in the *platía* (square) in Galáta if you want the keys to them.

The *Panagía Podíthou* church was built in 1502 as part of a monastery, which has since vanished without trace. The frescoes inside the church reveal strong Italian Renaissance influence, for instance in the façades forming the Italianate vedutà backdrop of numerous representations. Another example of Renaissance in-

MARCO POLO SELECTION: TRÓODOS

1 Ólympos
By car up the highest mountain in Cyprus (page 80)

2 Tróodos
Walk through beauties of nature (page 82)

3 Kykko Monastery
Still as prosperous as ever (page 78)

4 Hotel Linos
Luxury in a traditional village house (page 83)

5 Hotel Forest Park
Holidays at 1,500 m (page 83)

6 Psiló Déndro Restaurant
Trout fresh from the ponds (page 83)

spiration is the All Saints picture in the apse vault. A donor inscription is evidence that these frescoes were commissioned by a Frankish officer, who obviously chose an artist willing to paint the frescoes he donated to suit his Western taste.

Only a very short distance away is the much smaller *Archangels' church* (Archángeli) dating from 1514. Its frescoes are painted in a very rustic, vernacular style, not at all influenced by the Italian Renaissance, although here, too, the donor was a Frankish noble. He had a group portrait painted of himself with his family in a fresco below Christ enthroned.

Kakópetriá   (103/D4)

The name of this village means 'bad rock' in Greek. It abuts Galáta just below it. Even more Nicosíans and visitors come here in summer to cool off than to Galáta. The medieval core of the town, which is a protected historic monument, is strung out along a cliff squeezed between two streambeds in what amounts to a very narrow valley indeed (elevation 700 m).

Tree-shaded tavernas near an old watermill or in the spacious village square are the main attraction for those who would like to escape from the heat. On summer evenings the grill spits never stop turning to feed all those guests enjoying the cool night air.

Five km outside Kakópetriá there is a celebrated gem of Byzantine sacred art: the church of *Ágios Nikólaos tis Stégis,* 11th century *(Tues – Sat 9 am – 4 pm, Sun 11 am–4 pm, admission free).* The frescoes adorning its interior are world masterpieces of medieval art, dating from several centuries and representative of several different styles. The earliest frescoes are from the 11th century. These early figures are represented in hieratic poses with rigid facial expressions, as the Christ and other figures in the Entry into Jerusalem or the Raising of Lazarus show. By the 12th century, representations like the Forty Martyrs of Sebaste or the Judgement Day figures are more expressive in style although still stereotypical.

The mid-14th-century frescoes are in a lively vernacular style, exemplified by the Birth of Christ. Only doughty soldier-saints wearing chain mail and greaves decorated with lilies, such as St Theodore and St George (late 14th century), reveal some Western influence.

Kalopanagiótis   (102/C4)

The mountain village of Kalopanagiótis (elevation 750 m) is situated in the lower reaches of Marathása Valley. Hot sulphur springs very close by are a Cypriot spa but they are rarely interesting to visitors from abroad, who come all this way to see the former monastery of *Ágios Ioánnis Lampadistís* for its frescoes.

The monastery *(Mon – Sat 8 am – 12 noon and 1.30 pm – 5 pm, admission free)* stands on a slight elevation above the valley floor. Its fine frescoes date predominately from the 13th and 15th centuries. The monks' cells have been faithfully refurnished with antique agricultural implements, such as oil and wine presses. About 150 m below the monastery, sulphur springs bubble up from the right bank of the stream. You can drink the water if you like.

Kykko Monastery (102/B4)

★ Kykko is the most famous Cypriot monastery of all. Remote from human habitation, it is situated (elevation 1,140 m) on the slopes of Mount Kykko. Its forbiddingly austere façade conceals two cloisters with airy arcades and splendid mosaics on a gold ground. The church interior has just been completely decorated with frescoes.

A small museum, also owned by the monastery, houses centuries-old treasures appropriately exhibited.

All the monastery buildings, which were erected in 1813 after a devastating fire, are well maintained.

Because it is of major religious and historical importance, the monastery draws flocks of Cypriot pilgrims. In summer and at weekends throughout the year, it is thronged with visitors. On Sunday mornings many baptisms are celebrated at Kykko Monastery.

The most significant religious artefact in the monastery is an icon of the Virgin said to have been painted by Luke the Evangelist on a wooden panel given to him by an archangel for the purpose. The icon was presented to the monastery on its foundation in 1080 by the Byzantine emperor. Today the icon, encrusted with silver and gold,

The magnificently ornate portal of Kykko Monastery

hangs on the iconostasis and is credited with miraclulous powers. It has brought much needed rain to entire regions afflicted with drought. Grateful beneficiaries of its intercession have presented the monastery with enormous riches over the years. Now its material assets include hotels and manufacturing firms as well as a great deal of land on Cyprus. Hostels to accommodate pilgrims surround the monstery. It leases concessions to the proprietors of souvenir stalls and a restaurant at the monastery, considered the island's biggest. The 19th-century mosaics and frescoes further attest to great prosperity.

However, Kykko is not just a place of religious pilgrimage; it is also a national shrine visited by patriotic Greek Cypriots. General Grívas, the partisan leader of resistance against the British occupation, had his headquarters near the monastery. The monks never stinted with aid to the freedom fighters. One of the inhabitants of the monastery, Archbishop Makários III, was the spiritual leader of the Greek Cypriot resistance movement. His tomb is nearby. A good paved road winds up Mount Throní, 2 km away, where a military guard of honour watches over the Archbishop's tomb. Near it there is also a small chapel with a modern mosaic icon of the Virgin of Kykko. Pious visitors have tied scarves and handkerchiefs to the branches of a tree next to the chapel to enhance the efficacy of their prayers. *Monastery and tomb open during the day, admission free (museum 50c)*

Troodítissa Monastery (103/D6)

Compared with Kykko, Troodítissa seems a modest monastery indeed. Its monks eschew commerce, industry and politics, dedicating themselves instead to cultivating apple orchards and raising sheep and goats. The monastery church, consecrated in 1731, is renowned for a silver-mounted icon of the Virgin, whose intercession is sought by childless women longing to conceive. *Since 1998 non-Orthodox visitors have not been admitted to the monastery*

Kourdalí (103/E5)

Students of Byzantine art or holidaymakers who have developed a taste for it while in Cyprus might consider taking a detour to Kourdalí, just off the road from Kakopetriá to Tróodos. The church, consecrated to the Dormition, is reached via a Venetian bridge. It boasts some superb 16th-century frescoes. Both the iconostasis and the icons suspended from it are contemporaneous with the frescoes.

Lagouderá (104/A5)

Panagía tou Arakoú church on the outskirts of this peaceful mountain village in the eastern Tróodos is particularly fine. A domed building from the late 12th century, it was given an additional shed-like roof during the Crusader period in the characteristic Tróodos style. Here it reaches almost to the ground. The frescoes in the church were executed about 1200 by a master from the imperial capital of Constantinople. They exemplify the art of the Comnenian period, which reflects ancient Greek inspiration. The figures, especially the Christ in the dome, have been rendered in a remarkably dignified yet expressive style.

The village priest keeps the key to the church. You'll find him either in what was once a tract of the monastery next to the church or in a *kafeníon*. *Admission free, but please buy some postcards*

Louvarás (113/D1–2)

Lovers of Byzantine art shouldn't miss this village in the southern Tróodos. At its centre is the church of Ágios Mámas with frescoes dating from 1495. They are the work of the painter who executed the frescoes in the church of Stavrós tou Agiasmáti. Here the frescoes include representations of saints and scenes from the Passion as well as miracles performed by Christ. There are also double portraits of the two couples who were the donors of the church frescoes. *The key is kept in the house next to the second road sign in the village pointing to the church*

Monágri (112/B2)

Like so many other villages in the Tróodos, Monágri is definitely worth a visit if you happen to be a lover of Byzantine art. The village priest keeps the keys to three fine churches: Ágios Geórgios with late 15th-century frescoes, the church of the Archangel Michael decorated with 18th-century frescoes and, especially interesting, the church of Panagía Amasgoú, with frescoes executed between *c.* 1110 and 1564.

Moutoullás (102/C4)

◈ The fertile Marathása Valley, renowned throughout Cyprus for its 90,000 cherry trees, is at an elevation of 800 m. Here a large village is keeping old traditions alive. Carpenters and joiners still make the troughs in which bread used to be kneaded and long boards grooved with depressions in which bread was carried to communal ovens to be baked. On the terraces of several houses in this village, a local speciality, *Joujoúko*, is cooked and dried, a sausage-shaped Cypriot delicacy made of grape must and nuts. A spring in the village provides water which is bottled and marketed across Cyprus under the name of Moutoullás. Take the time for a rewarding stroll through the village. For those who cannot bear to miss even one church, Panagía tou Moutoullás conceals some frescoes dating from 1280, but they are in a very sad state of preservation. *Key in house next to church*

Ólympos (103/D5)

★ ⊌ The highest peak on Cyprus (1,951 m), Ólympos is a mountain you can drive up. On its twin peaks stand British military aerials and a tall Cypriot television relay station, which are visible from a great distance so you know which mountain is Ólympos. The peak affords panoramic views across to the Kyrénia Mountains and Nicosía, the Mesaoría plain and Mórfou Bay as well as Kykko Monastery and Pródromos, Mount Kiónia above Machairás Monastery and the sparse stands of trees at timberline. Between January and

March they are usually blanketed with deep snow. Well marked footpaths lead off the paved road between the peak and the town of Tróodos so that you can go off on foot in any direction you choose without committing yourself to a strenuous hike.

Ómodos   (112/A1)

This is a wine-growing village on the slopes across from Páno Plátres. At the lower end of the pretty village square, there is an abandoned monastery. The church associated with it preserves a relic of the Apostle Philip's skull as well as pieces of the True Cross and the ropes with which Christ was bound. Memorabilia are exhibited in what was once the monastery chapterhouse commemorating the freedom fighters, many of whom used the monastery as a refuge between 1955 and 1958. The chapterhouse has a remarkable wooden ceiling. Other rooms house antique agricultural implements and domestic utensils.

Near the monastery you can visit several traditional houses, two antique wine-presses, which have been accorded historic monument status, and the studio of the woman who executed the modern glass windows of the monastery church. The Ólympos wine cellars on the outskirts of the village are a further attraction, open *Mon–Fri from 10 am–4 pm* to visitors.

Palaikhóri   (104/B5)

Virtually unspoilt by tourism, this village on the road from Nicosía to Límassol via Agrós boasts two churches with beautiful frescoes you shouldn't miss. The church of the Metamórfosis is on a hill above the town. Its interior is full of early 16th-century frescoes in an excellent state of preservation. One of the most interesting representations is a prefiguration of the Last Supper with Abraham entertaining three angels at a semicircular table. A goat is suckling her kid in front of the table.

Panagía Chrysopantánassa in the village square is a church concealing four 16th-century frescoes, which unfortunately have not been cleaned so that they are extremely difficult to make out.

Ask the village priest if you want to have the church key.

Páno Plátres   (103/D6)

This mountain resort (elevation 1,100 m) is cool in summer. With numerous hotels and tavernas, it is the tourist hub of the Tróodos Mountains. At midsummer and during the January-February skiing season the place is as packed as the coastal resorts. Páno Plátres is a good starting point for trips to the rest of the Tróodos, although the village offers no special attractions for sightseers.

Pedoulás   (102/C5)

Pedoulás (elevation 1,170) at the head of the Marathása Valley is a large village set in cherry orchards. Although corrugated tin roofs detract from the charm of the village, lovers of Byzantine art will find compensation in Archangel Michael Church with its shed-like roof. Near the modern church in the lower village, it boasts late 15th-century frescoes. Ask for the key next door or get it from the village priest.

Pródromos (103/D5)

Named after John the Baptist ('forerunner'), this is the island's highest (1,400 m) village inhabited all year round.

Stavrós tou Agiasmáti (104/A4)

Remote from human habitation in the wooded mountains of the eastern Tróodos, there is a tiny church with the distinctive roof that is a regional feature: Stavrós tis Agiasmáti. Look in the *kafeníons* at Platanistássa 4 km away for the man who keeps the key so that you can view the remarkable interior with its frescoes. The most important of these are in a niche on the wall to your left. Dating from the 15th century, one narrative sequence of scenes represents the conversion of the Roman Emperor Constantine the Great to Christianity while a second depicts the finding of the True Cross by his mother, Helena.

Tróodos (103/D5)

★ Just below Mount Ólympos there is a little holiday resort at an elevation of 1,700 m. Nearly every visitor to the Tróodos takes a break here. There are several tavernas, two hotels, a campingsite and stables with horses for hire as well as tennis courts here. In winter you can even rent skis on the path from Tróodos up the side of Ólympos.

◁▷ At Tróodos an instructively labelled nature trail goes almost all the way round Mount Ólympos at an elevation of 1,700 m. Highly informative on plants and geological phenomena, it affords superb views as well. It runs for 12 km before joining the Pródromos-Tróodos road so that you can walk the last 4 km back to Tróodos on it. Taking the nature trail is not at all strenuous because its gradient is such that it is virtually level all the way. You won't need more than tennis shoes or other light footwear. At the start, you may find brochures in various languages describing what you'll see along the way. However, it's advisable to send to the Cyprus Tourism Organization office in your country for a brochure before you leave home.

RESTAURANTS

The mountains are well provided with restaurants. There are lots of places to eat in Kakopetriá, Páno Plátres and Tróodos. You'll also find restaurants at Kykko Monastery and in Ómodos, Pedoulás, Pródromos and Agrós.

There are more eateries on the main roads through the mountains. Three restaurants here deserve special mention:

Danae (103/D4)

An unassuming taverna whose speciality is *skeftaliá* wrapped in pitta bread. *Daily from 9 am, Kakopetriá Platía (square), category 3*

Maryland (103/D4)

A beautifully appointed and kept up restaurant in a highly unconventional building at the old watermill. Magnificent views! *Daily from 12 noon, Kakopetriá, category 2*

A will of her own

Like so many monastic foundations on Cyprus, Troodítissa was inspired by a miraculous icon. Hermits had discovered the icon of the Virgin 1,000 years ago in a cave and began at once to build a chapel on the spot where it was found. However, whatever they built during the day was mysteriously demolished overnight. The icon disappeared more than once, only to be found by the pious hermits invariably in the same place: a well where the present monastery now stands. It gradually dawned on them that this was where the Virgin wanted her church to be built. The miracle drew even more pious hermits to Troodítissa and thus was the community of monks established.

Psiló Déndro (103/D6)

★ Near Páno Plátres with a fireplace and large garden shaded by great sycamores; delicious trout raised in the restaurant's own ponds. *Daily 9 am – 4 pm, open longer mid-summer, category 2*

HOTELS

Forest Park (103/D6)

★ Best hotel in the Tróodos, English ambience. *137 rooms, Páno Plátres, Tel. 02 / 42 17 51, Fax 42 18 75, category 1*

Jack's (102/C5)

Unpretentious inn. *20 rooms, Pedoulás, Tel. 02 / 95 23 50, Fax 95 28 17, category 3*

Jubilee (103/D5)

Hotel above town of Tróodos on the road to Mount Ólympos. *37 rooms, Tróodos, Tel. 05 / 42 16 47, Fax 42 16 28, category 2*

Linos 103/D4)

★ Ten rooms in Cypriot style, some with jacuzzi, in stone houses that are on a protected national heritage site. *Kakopetriá, Tel. 02 / 92 31 61, Fax 92 31 81, categories 1 and 2*

Pendéli (103/D6)

Hotel with all modern amenities and a pool, located at centre of town. *81 rooms, Páno Plátres, Tel. 05 / 42 17 36, Fax 42 18 08, category 2*

Rialto (103/D4)

Unassuming hotel located where Galáta merges with Kakopetriá. *29 rooms, Galáta, Tel. 02 / 92 24 38, category 3*

Rodon (104/A5–6)

A modern hotel with pool, which is owned and run by a cooperative of village residents. *155 rooms, Agrós, Tel. 05 / 52 12 01, Fax 52 12 35, category 2*

Tróodos Sunotel (103/D5)

Completly modernized in 1989, the hotel is in the tiny town centre of Tróodos (elevation 1,700 m). *48 rooms, Tróodos, Tel. 05 / 42 16 35, Fax 42 25 00, category 2*

INFORMATION

Cyprus Tourism Organization (103/D6)

Páno Plátres, centre of town, Tel. 05 / 42 13 16, Apr – Oct only

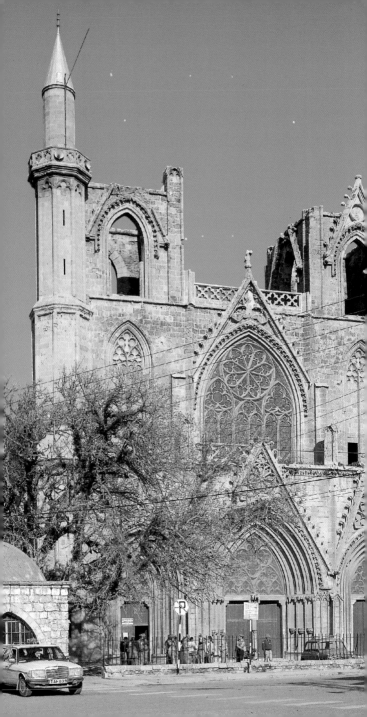

The other part of the island

Tourists can also visit the Turkish-occupied north of the Republic of Cyprus

FAMAGÚSTA

(109/D2) ★ Until the 1974 Turkish invasion, Famagústa (Ammókostos) was the island's most important port. Then it had all the hotels in Cyprus. Since 1964 the old town had been a purely Turkish-Cypriot residential section under UN protection. The modern hotel city of Varósha (Varóches), on the other hand, was exclusively Greek-Cypriot.

In the Middle Ages Famagústa was an even more important city than Nicosía. It had a population of over 70,000 in the 14th century. The trade with Asia Minor and the Near East, which centred on the port of Famagústa, brought the city unparalleled prosperity. Its nobles grew so rich that they became the donors of numerous large churches. You can still see these Gothic ruins, which add a delicate touch of filigree tracery to the city's maze of Oriental-

Lala Mustafa Mosque in Famagústa is an impressive sight

looking bazaar alleys and the minarets added to all Christian churches when they were converted into mosques.

SIGHTS

Lala Mustafa Mosque
Ninety years after construction had begun on Nicosía's Gothic cathedral and shortly after the expulsion of the last Crusaders from the Holy Land, the Frankish kingdom of Cyprus was so prosperous that the cornerstone for a second cathedral was laid, this time in Famagústa. It was built in only 28 years and consecrated at the same time as the Cathedral of St Sophia in Nicosía (1326). The church at Famagústa is Gothic throughout with a splendid west façade recalling French Gothic cathedrals at their most magnificent. A low minaret is the only external indication that Famagústa Cathedral was converted into a mosque in 1571.

Othello Tower
◊◊ In the Middle Ages a citadel incorporated into the fortification

walls guarded Famagústa harbour. Since the days of British colonial rule, it has been called the Othello Tower because the Shakespearean tragedy was set in Cyprus. It is not hard to imagine this little fort as the place where Othello murdered his wife Desdemona. From the roof you have the most beautiful views across the old town of Famagústa.

RESTAURANTS

There are several unassuming restaurants in the old town of Famagústa, which usually accept only Turkish lira in payment. However, we recommend the restaurant at the entrance to the excavation at Salamís for a pleasant break at noon. You can sit by the sea there.

SURROUNDING AREA

St Barnabas Monastery
(Moní Apostólou Várnava) (108/C1)
The Apostle Barnabas, who accompanied St Paul on his mission to Cyprus, was, as legend has it, murdered at Salamís. In 477 Anthémios, Archbishop of Cyprus, found the saint's grave. This historic discovery led to the recognition of an independent Cypriot national church soon thereafter. A small modern chapel now stands over the Apostle's grave about 100 m below the Monastery of St Barnabas, which is thought to have been founded in the 5th century. The monastery church dates back to the 10th century although it was rebuilt in the 18th century. *8 km from Famagústa*

Salamís (109/D1)
★ You'll get the best idea of just how vast ancient Salamís was from the very top tiers of seats in the Roman amphitheatre, where 15,000 spectators could sit. Another impressive sight is the Roman-Early Christian palaestra, that is, the colonnade and floors of the ancient wrestling school. An ancient communal latrine, which accommodated

MARCO POLO SELECTION: NORTH CYPRUS

1 Famagústa
Time has stood still in the old town (page 85)

2 Salamís
An archaeological park right on the sea (page 86)

3 Keryneia
The harbour is the most beautiful place to sit in Cyprus (page 87)

4 Shipwreck Museum
A 2,300-year-old trading boat and its cargo (page 88)

5 Bellapais
Romantic Gothic Augustine Abbey (page 88)

6 Ágios Ilárion
A Byzantine castle like an eagle's eyrie (page 88)

Keryneia harbour and castle look back on a turbulent history

44 men, has been preserved. Far apart from each other on the site are the walls of two Early Christian basilicas and an ancient Zeus temple.

Outside the fenced-in excavation site are some striking mounds on the left-hand side of the road to St Barnabas Monastery. They belong to an ancient necropolis, with graves that, unlike the city ruins, are not Roman but date from the 7th and 6th centuries BC. The finds are in the Nicosía Cyprus Museum. Gruesomely well preserved *in situ* are the skeletons of chariot horses sacrificed, as in Homer, to accompany their noble masters in death. *8 km from Famagústa*

KERYNEIA

(**O**) Only 45 minutes' drive from Nicosía across the narrow ridge of the Kyrénia Mountains lies the loveliest city in Cyprus, now called Girne in Turkish.

It is centred on the tiny, almost perfectly semicircular Venetian harbour. It is fringed with cafés and restaurants against a backdrop of centuries-old houses. A massive fortress dominates one side of the harbour. Slender church spires and minarets rise from the old town. Just behind the city the ground rises steeply to the mountains. The peaks of the Pendedáktylos Range look spectacularly Alpine. Here in the north the narrow strip of coastal plain is verdant with glossy lemon and orange groves.

Near Keryneia, the village of Bellapais nestles on the slopes. It is renowned for the romantic ruins of a Gothic abbey. The Crusader fortress of St Hilarion is just off the road to Nicosía below the crest of the ridge. Even a day trip reveals the breathtaking beauty of this stretch of the north coast. *25 km from Nicosía*

SIGHTS

Castle
Built in the Byzantine era, the castle looming over the harbour was enlarged by the Franks and then by the Venetians to keep up with developments in military science. From its walls

you have the best views across Keryneia and the mountains behind it.

Harbour
★ Byzantine, Crusader and Venetian ships have all lain at anchor in Keryneia harbour. Right in the harbour entrance are the ruins of a tower. In the Middle Ages a chain could be stretched between it to what is now the Customs House to keep out unwelcome visitors from across the sea.

Icon Museum
After the 1974 Turkish invasion, many works of Christian art were smuggled out of Cyprus and sold to unscrupulous foreign collectors. Archaeologists managed to outwit the looters and safeguard quite a few icons by hiding them in museum magazines. Since 1990 they have been on display in the Archángelos church in the old town of Keryneia.

Shipwreck Museum
★ A trading boat sank 2,300 years ago off Keryneia. Twenty years ago archaeologists lifted the wreck and its cargo from the seabed. The plank boat was over 4 m wide and over 14 m long. Its cargo enabled scholars to trace the route of its last voyage. The 400 wine amphorae on board came from Samos and Cos. In addition, 29 stone querns for grinding grain and even 9,000 well-preserved almonds were recovered. The finds are exhibited in the castle museum. *Daily 8am – 5.30 pm*

The restaurants round lovely Keryneia harbour are excellent places to take a midday break. They even accept Cypriot pounds as well as Turkish lires. You can also grab a quick snack right at Bellapais Abbey, where superb views across the coastal plain heighten the Gothic romance of the famous ruins.

Ágios Ilárion (O)
★ ↝ From the peaks of the Kyrénia Mountains you can see across to the Turkish coast on clear days. The proximity of the Asia Minor coast led the Byzantines to build a chain of forts across the mountains from which they could guard the approaches to Cyprus from the sea. The biggest and best preserved of these castles is Ágios Ilárion. You should plan to spend at least an hour exploring this spectacular fortress. *Daily 8.30 am – 4.30 pm, 10 km from Keryneia*

Bellapais (O)
★ Before the 1974 invasion, this beautiful mountain village was inhabited by Greek Cypriots. It can still be proud of owning the most spectacularly romantic ruin on the island. In 1205 Augustine monks founded an abbey that soon became rich and powerful. The magnificent pointed arches of what was once the cloister are proof of this, as are the large, perfectly preserved refectory and the Gothic cellars. *Daily 8 am – 6 pm, 5 km from Keryneia*

Discover the diversity of Cyprus on day trips

These routes are marked in green on the map on the inside front cover and in the Road Atlas beginning on page 99

① A DAY IN THE TRÓODOS MOUNTAINS

The only way to explore Cyprus in all its diversity is to spend at least a full day in the mountains. You'll find peaceful villages, beautiful valleys, unique churches and monasteries and have a bird's-eye view of Cyprus from Mt Ólympos. Round trip from Límassol and back: approx. 175 km. Time needed: at least 10 – 12 hours.

If you're an early riser, you can leave in a hire car for a day trip through the Tróodos Mountains from any place you happen to be staying on Cyprus. However, if you prefer just rolling over and going back to sleep at dawn, you'd be better off starting this tour from Límassol or Pissoúri. You leave Límassol via motorway exit 28 on a well constructed country road going up into the mountains. The road signs point to *Plátres.* You pass two reservoirs, and *Mount Ólympos* is by now clearly in your sights. You certainly can't miss

the white radar dome and the red-and-white television relay station standing on its twin peaks. Terraced vineyards line the road. The grapes that are cultivated here are used in making sweet *commandaría* wine unique to Cyprus. Then at *Lánia* you might take your first break. On the right side of the road, in the garden of the *Royal Oak Tree* café, there is a centuries-old Portuguese oak, which is 17 m tall and 6 m across. An unusual lookout platform has been built on its branches. The village above the road, *Lánia (p. 47),* is worth taking time to see on foot (drive up to it and park). Here you can watch several artists and craftsmen at their work and buy things they make if you like them.

Not long past *Trimíklini* the road suddenly forks. The road to the left is the quicker route to Plátres; the road to the right leads to Kakopetriá and Nicosía. If you turn off towards Nicosía and then, at the top of the pass, turn again towards Tróodos, you'll drive past what was once a vast opencast mining operation. Here asbestos was mined and worked well into the 1980s. The road now winds tortuously uphill through sparsely wooded slopes. The tree species endemic to this region are the holm-oak, the black pine and the strawberry tree. At 1,700 m, you'll reach the hamlet of *Tróodos*, where another road goes all the way up the mountain you've been looking at, *Ólympos*, with the television relay station on top. You see far across the *Mesaoría plain*, all the way to the *Kyrénia Mountains*, the *Bay of Mórfou* and a monastery, *Kykko*.

Now you have to completely circumnavigate Ólympos. To do so, you first drive on to *Pródromos*, from there to the remote monastery called *Troodítissa* and then to the mountain resort of *Páno Plátres (p. 81)*.

In this bracing air, enjoy fresh trout in the cool *Psiló Déndro (p. 83)* restaurant under shady trees. However, you should save that cup of coffee afterwards for the wine-growing village of *Ómodos (p. 81)*, which you reach by driving first of all through *Páno Plátres*, on down to *Káto Plátres* and finally through *Mandriá*. After visiting the monastery and strolling through romantic alleys, you'll relish the delicious coffee served in the island's most beautiful *platía*.

The road down from Ómodos to the coast again goes through spectacular unspoilt scenery, if, all the way down, you follow the river valley of the *Diárizos*. The valley is almost without human habitation except for a few deserted, formerly Turkish-Cypriot hamlets, some still lived in by a shepherd and his wife. Huge flocks of sheep and goats move across the green slopes. Villages along the road with *kafeníons* rarely visited by tourists are *Ágios Nikólaos, Mamónia* and *Fasoúla*. Two km west of *Koúklia* you turn back on to the old coast road. Either continue on it or take the motorway, which is to be finished in 1999, on back to where you're staying.

② MEMORABLE SCENERY AND HISTORIC PLACES IN THE FAR WEST

 Páfos and the surrounding region are the native country of Aphrodite, the goddess of love. Spending a day tracing her footsteps in your hire car is a rewarding experience. You won't find just ruined temples, churches and a monastery. What also awaits you is variegated coastal scenery and diverse flora. Distance from the Rocks of Aphrodite to Páfos: approx. 140 km. Time needed: at least 9 – 10 hours.

Páfos is the best starting point for this tour. However, you can do it in reverse by starting at Pólis. From the south, you depart from the *Rocks of Aphrodite (p. 70)*, called by Cypriots *Pétra tou Romeoú*. This is the mythical place where the ancient Greek goddess of love is supposed to have emerged from the sea foam and to have first set foot on terra firma. The coast road leads west from this idyllic spot through the broad fertile coastal plain of Páfos. After about ten minutes' drive, you'll have no trouble spotting a little fort perched on the top of a low mesa: *Covôcle*, marking the site of the Aphrodite sanctuary at *Palaiá Páfos*, which is the first place you'll probably want to stop and explore. The museum is also worth a visit. From here you will drive on to *Geroskípou*. In the village square right on the main road, there is a very old-looking church: *Agía Paraskeví*, a six-domed structure. The name of the village means 'of the sacred grove'. Where the church now stands there was an altar set in a lovely garden. Votaries on their way from Páfos to the Aphrodite sanctuary stopped there to sacrifice to the love goddess.

Páfos (p. 64) is a place you must spend an entire day in. That is why our route bypasses the city and goes on towards *Pólis*. Beyond Páfos take a short detour to the venerable monastery of *Ágios Neófytos (p. 71)*, a chapel in the rock decorated throughout with frescoes. Here the contrast to the ancient gods, with their exuberant hedonism, is sharp indeed. The austere Christian saint venerated in the grotto lived an ascetic life, eschewing earthly pleasures.

From here the main road continues for a while uphill through slopes covered with carob trees, whose pods are standard fodder for sheep and goats, before giving way to vineyards. Then it goes down again, straight to the north coast, through orange groves and tobacco fields until you reach the small town of *Pólis (p. 73)*. Here or in neighbouring *Lákki (Látchi; p. 72)* you'll enjoy a swim and take a welcome midday break.

Afterwards your route goes on through lovely coastal scenery to

where the road ends in the west at the quite romantically named *Aphrodite's Bath (p. 69)*. Legend has it that the goddess of love had secret trysts with her lover, Akamas, at this secluded spring-fed pond. The westernmost peninsula of Cyprus is named after him.

To return to the south coast, you may want to try an alternative route via a few villages still relatively untouched by tourism, such as *Droúseia (Droúsha)* and *Káthikas*. With the lights twinkling in Páfos down below, the evening drive from Káthikas via the village of *Pégeia* is really breathtaking. This is the view enjoyed by pilots landing at Páfos Airport. Down in Páfos once more, relax over a bottle of chilled white wine – Aphrodite is a brand that springs to mind.

③ EXCURSIONS IN THE LÁRNAKA AREA

 If you're staying round Lárnaka and Agía Nápa for your holidays, this is just the day trip for you in your hire car. The route combines a variety of exciting things to do yet still leaves you with plenty of time for a refreshing swim and some leisurely shopping. Distance round trip from Lárnaka and back: approx. 150 km. Time needed: at least 9 – 10 hours.

You start off heading for Límassol on the motorway, which you stay on until you reach exit 13. From there a very well constructed road leads up into the southern outliers of the *Tróodos Mountains* to the big village of *Páno Léfkara*. It is world-famous for drawn-work lace and silver filigree work. You can buy both in any of numerous shops in town here. Then you drive on via the small village of *Káto Drys*, which has an authentic Cypriot *kafeníon*, right on down into a mountain valley encircled with hills to the convent of *Ágios Minás (p. 38)* at the centre. Here you can watch a nun paint icons. If your heart is set on purchasing an icon, you can order one and have it sent to you. Then via *Vávla* you'll leave the valley once again and continue on down to famous *Choirokoitía (p. 37)*, where the best preserved Late Neolithic settlement on Cyprus has been excavated, to your left on the slope just before the motorway exit. People lived here in houses with stone footings 9,000 years ago. From here head towards Límassol on the motorway and leave it at exit 17. A side road leads to the beaches known as *Governor's Beach*, with great tavernas and scenery as yet hardly marred by development.

After a midday break, you can then head for Nicosía on the motorway, leaving it at exit 11 to drive up to the conical, crosstopped mountain of *Stavrovoní*, an important monastery that, don't forget, admits men only. Afterwards you drive back a way towards the motorway exit and then continue on a good secondary road towards the quiet village of *Pyrgá (p. 39)*. After visiting the Royal Chapel there, you continue on the road through a forest, which soon gives way to a bizarre landscape of reddish and white mesas, to pass through the town of *Kalókhorió* and finally reach Lárnaka. By now you will have had a truly memorable day.

④ FROM THE CAPITAL INTO REMOTE FASTNESSES

This is a day trip to spirit you away in your hire car from the bustle of the metropolis to restful solitude in the eastern outliers of the Tróodos. There you'll find the perfect blend of culture and natural beauty. Take a picnic hamper with you: there are no tavernas here.

Round trip from Nicosía and back again: approx. 100 km. Time needed: at least 7 - 8 hours.

To get out of Nicosía, first follow the signs for Stróvolos and then the ones for Lakatámeia. After driving through Lakatámeia, you will reach the large village of *Káto Deftéra*. Perched on the cliffs north of the village you'll see the church of *Panagía Chrysospiliótissa*, which you can climb up to. In *Péra* a road branches off to the town of *Politikó*. There you should look at the Royal Tombs of ancient Tamassós and visit a convent with a lovely garden. The nuns here make and sell marzipan.

Then you go on via *Kampiá* right up into the mountains to *Machairás Monastery (p. 60)*, entirely secluded in thick woods at an elevation of 900 m. From here you drive on to the deserted mountain village of *Lazaniás* nearly all the way to *Goúrri*, where a new road goes up to *Fikárdou (p. 58)*. The whole village is a protected historic monument and an open-air museum of life on Cyprus 60 years ago.

You will now drive back via *Goúrri* and *Klírou* on down into the Mesaoría plain and through *Káto Deftéra* to reach the island capital of Nicosía.

Practical information

*Important addresses and useful information
for your visit to Cyprus*

AMERICAN & BRITISH ENGLISH

The Marco Polo travel guides are written in British English. In North America, certain terms and usages deviate from British usage. Some of the more frequently encountered examples are:
baggage for luggage, billion for milliard, cab for taxi, car rental for car hire, drugstore for chemist's, fall for autumn, first floor for groundfloor, freeway/highway for motorway, gas(oline) for petrol, railroad for railway, restroom for toilet/lavatory, streetcar for tram, subway for underground/tube, toll-free numbers for freephone numbers, trailer for caravan, trunk for boot, vacation for holidays, wait staff for waiting staff (in restaurants etc.), zip code for postal code.

ANIMALS

Animals are quarantined for six months before they may be brought into the Republic of Cyprus.

BANKS & CURRENCY

The unit of currency in the Republic of Cyprus is the Cyprus pound or lira in Greek (abbreviated CYP). A pound has 100 cents. There are no restrictions on bringing CYP, foreign currency in banknotes or travellers' cheques into Cyprus. Eurocheques can be cashed at all banks and most major international credit cards are accepted in the larger shops, hotels and restaurants. Banks are open Mon – Fri 8.30 am – 12 noon. In the main cities, towns and tourist centres, some banks are also open 3.30 pm – 5.30 pm (Oct – Apr) and 4 pm – 6 pm (May – Sept). Round-the-clock banking service is available at Larnaca and Páfos International Airports.

CAMPING

There are seven official campsites on Cyprus: Agía Nápa (Mar – Oct), Geroskípou (Apr – Oct), Governor's Beach (all year round), Lárnaka (June – Oct), Páfos (all year round), Pólis (Mar – Oct) and Tróodos (May – Oct). The normal daily charge is between CYP 1.25 and 1.50 per tent space and person. Camping on unauthorized grounds is officially prohibited but this is often ignored by the locals.

CAR HIRE

Cars, mopeds and motorbikes are available for hire at all tourist centres. There is a shortage of cars during the summer months so book one well in advance. All you need to hire a car is your country's driving licence.

Prices: small cars CYP 10–15 per day, depending on the season, with unlimited mileage; mopeds from CYP 4 a day and bicycles from CYP 2 a day (see also DRIVING).

CUSTOMS

Adult visitors may take the following in and out of Cyprus duty-free: 200 cigarettes or 250 g tobacco, 1 litre of spirits and 2 litres of wine per person.

There is no limit to the amount of currency you may bring into Cyprus, but amounts exceeding $1,000 or the equivalent must be declared.

DIPLOMATIC & CONSULAR OFFICES

English-speaking countries:

British High Commission of the Republic of Cyprus:
93 Park Street London W1Y 4ET; Tel. 01 71 / 4 99 82 72 / 4

Embassy of the Republic of Cyprus (USA)
2211 R Street North West, Washington, DC, Tel. 2 02 / 46 25 72 / 08 73

British High Commission:
*Alexándrou Pállis Street,
PO Box
1978 Nicosía,
Tel. 02 / 47 31 31 / 7*

United States Embassy
*Metóchiou and Ploutárchou Streets, Nicosía,
Tel. 02 / 47 61 00*

Canadian Embassy
*Margaret House, 15 Od. Them. Dervi, Nicosía,
Tel. 02 / 45 16 30*

DRIVING

Cars may be brought into Cyprus for up to three months duty- and tax-free. If you plan to stay longer, you may apply for an extension at the Customs Office in Nicosía. Make sure your insurance covers you on Cyprus. There are ferry connections from Piraeus.

ELECTRICITY

240 volts AC. Many modern buildings have sockets for British three square-pin plugs.

EMERGENCIES

Ambulance, police, fire, night pharmacies: *dial 199.*

INFORMATION

Cyprus Tourism Organization (CTO)
Informations about Cyprus can be obtained from the following offices of the Cyprus Tourism Organization (CTO): www.cyprustourism.org

*United Kingdom CTO: 213 Regent Street, London W1R 8DA, Tel. 01 71 / 7 34 98 22 / 25 93
United States CTO: 13 East 40th Street, New York, NY 10016, Tel. 2 12 / 6 83 52 80
CTO Head Office: PO Box 4535, 19 Límassol Avenue, Nicosía (postal enquiries)*

CTO personal and telephone enquiries: Laikí Gitoniá, Nicosía, Tel. 02 / 44 42 64
There are CTO branches in the following major towns: Límassol, Lárnaka, Páfos, Agía Nápa, Plátres and Tróodos (see relevant chapters for details).

MEASURES & WEIGHTS

1 cm	0.39 inch
1 m	1.09 yd (3.28 ft)
1 km	0.62 miles
1 m²	1.20 yd²
1 ha	2.47 acres
1 km²	0.39 mi²
1 g	0.035 ounces
1 kg	2.21 pounds
British ton	*1016 kg*
US ton	*907 kg*

1 litre is equivalent to 0.22 Imperial gallons and 0.26 US gallons

MEDICAL SERVICES

Medical services on Cyprus are very good. Many doctors trained in Great Britain or North America. Most speak excellent English.

You are urgently advised to take out a private health-insurance policy in your home country prior to departing for Cyprus as you will be expected to pay for treatment and medicine in cash. Emergency calls (ambulance, police, fire brigade, night pharmacies): 199.

NEWSPAPERS, RADIO & TV

The daily *Cyprus Mail* and the *Cyprus Weekly* are published in English. UK newspapers sold in cities and tourist centres are two days late. The Cyprus Broadcasting Corporation (CyBC) broadcasts in English on Channel 2 (498m/693kHz and 91.1 MHz

VHF). In summer a tourist programme called 'Welcome to Cyprus' is broadcast.

NORTH CYPRUS

You're on your own if you venture into the Turkish-occupied part of the island. The only place you can cross the border is at the old Ledra Palace Hotel checkpoint. Only here can you find out whether the border is open when you want to cross. You can only cross on foot (to the north until 1 pm and back by 6 pm). Staying overnight in the occupied part and bringing purchases made there into the free part are forbidden by the Greek-Cypriot authorities. The Turkish-Cypriot authorities will issue a visa valid for a day for a fee of CYP 1. Do not let your passport be stamped or you cannot return to the free part of Cyprus. The unit of currency in the Turkish-occupied part is the Turkish lira. You can easily cover north Nicosía on foot. Taxis for other destinations in the occupied part of Cyprus wait north of the checkpoint.

NUDISM

Nudism is officially prohibited on Republic of Cyprus beaches and Cypriots find it offensive. Ladies are, nonetheless, seen topless on beaches and at the poolside.

PASSPORTS & VISAS

Holders of valid US or EU passports don't need visas for stays of up to three months, however it is necessary to obtain a permit to stay longer. Children must be entered in a parent's or guardian's passport.

With a stamp in your passport from Turkish-occupied north Cyprus, you won't be admitted to the Republic of Cyprus by the Greek-Cypriot authorities.

PHOTOGRAPHY & FILMING

You are permitted to photograph and film at archaeological excavation sites without paying a fee but you must apply in writing several days in advance for an official permit to photograph in public museums. Photographing or filming military installations is strictly forbidden and this also applies to the Green Line in Nicosía. If you are caught, your film will be confiscated by the authorities.

POST & TELEPHONE SERVICES

Telephone calls can be made from coin and phonecard operated call-boxes in large towns and most villages. Phonecards are available for CYP 3, 5 and 10 from kiosks, in many shops and at CTO offices. International dialling codes are: UK 0044; Eire 00353; USA and Canada 001; Australia 0061; New Zealand 0064. All country codes are followed by the city or town code minus the initial zero, e.g. London 0044 171.

The dialling code for calls to Cyprus from abroad is 357. The dialling codes for the main cities are: Nicosía 02; Agía Nápa 03; Lárnaka 04; Límassol 05; Páfos 06. For cellular phones: 09.

The postal and telephone services are separate entities. Post office opening times: Mon-Fri 7.30 am – 1 pm, Sat only to 12 noon; main post offices at Nicosía, Lárnaka, Límassol and Páfos Mon-Fri also 4 pm – 6 pm.

PUBLIC TRANSPORT

The cheapest form of public transport is the bus. Service buses connect all large towns and villages but there is a catch: services to villages usually operate only once daily. Buses leave villages for towns early in the morning and return in the evening. A viable alternative to buses is the *dolmus* or Service Taxi. Providing a service link between the main towns, these cars seat up to seven passengers and are usually scheduled to run every half-hour. You telephone to reserve a seat and arrange where you'll be collected and, at your destination, you'll be dropped wherever you want. Buses and Service Taxis operate only during the day, buses on weekdays and Service Taxis also on Sundays, albeit infrequently.

There is no shortage of urban taxis in towns, resorts and even some villages in the south. All vehicles are equipped with meters and fares are reasonable: the trip between Lárnaka and Nicosía (50 km) costs CYP 1.50 by bus, CYP 2.50 by *dolmus* and by regular taxi CYP 13. A 15 – 25 % surcharge is added to taxi fares between 11 pm and 5 am.

TIME

Cyprus is two hours ahead of Greenwich Mean Time (GMT). In summer clocks are put forward one hour. Summer Time is in force from the last weekend in March to the last weekend in September.

TIPPING

Restaurant and hotel bills include a 10 % service charge and 8 % VAT. However, if you have been given particularly good service, an extra tip of between 5 % and 10 % is the norm.

TRAFFIC REGULATIONS

Driving is on the left in Cyprus. On roundabouts, traffic coming from the right has priority. Speed limit in towns is 50 km/h, on country roads 80 km/h, on motorways 100 km/h.

WATER

Tap water is safe to drink over the island although in the larger towns and more densely populated areas it doesn't taste good.

YOUTH HOSTELS

Youth hostels mean basics only. To stay there you will need an International Youth Hostel Federation card. Hostels are in Agía Nápa, Lárnaka, Nicosía, Páfos, Stavrós tis Psókas and Tróodos. Prices: CYP 3.50 – 5.00 per person per night.

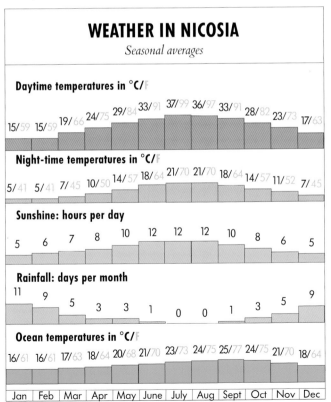

WEATHER IN NICOSIA

Seasonal averages

Daytime temperatures in °C/F

Jan	Feb	Mar	Apr	May	June	July	Aug	Sept	Oct	Nov	Dec
15/59	15/59	19/66	24/75	29/84	33/91	37/99	36/97	33/91	28/82	23/73	17/63

Night-time temperatures in °C/F

Jan	Feb	Mar	Apr	May	June	July	Aug	Sept	Oct	Nov	Dec
5/41	5/41	7/45	10/50	14/57	18/64	21/70	21/70	18/64	14/57	11/52	7/45

Sunshine: hours per day

Jan	Feb	Mar	Apr	May	June	July	Aug	Sept	Oct	Nov	Dec
5	6	7	8	10	12	12	12	10	8	6	5

Rainfall: days per month

Jan	Feb	Mar	Apr	May	June	July	Aug	Sept	Oct	Nov	Dec
11	9	5	3	3	1	0	0	1	3	5	9

Ocean temperatures in °C/F

Jan	Feb	Mar	Apr	May	June	July	Aug	Sept	Oct	Nov	Dec
16/61	16/61	17/63	18/64	20/68	21/70	23/73	24/75	25/77	24/75	21/70	18/64

Do's and don'ts

*How to avoid some of the traps and pitfalls
awaiting the unwary traveller*

Street gambling

During feasts and festivals and at open-air markets, you'll see card-sharps and tricksters operating on street corners. Ignore them even if you speak Greek.

Nudism

Nudism is officially forbidden and disapproved of in Cyprus. It is disgraceful that tourists have to be reminded to enter churches and monasteries properly clothed.

Cruises

Travel agents and tour operators in some Cypriot hotels are keen to make you sign up for a short cruise to the Holy Land or Egypt. Don't be tempted. Cyprus has so much to offer that you'd be sorry to leave sooner than you have to anyway. Moreover, the time you would have on shore in Israel and Cairo is too short and the tour guides who approach you at either destination are more interested in selling you souvenirs than in showing you around.

Discounts/Sales

At Páno Léfkara you'll be made to believe that you have arrived just in time for the sales, with a 10 % or more reduction offered everywhere you go. This happens all year round and is just a way of fooling tourists into thinking they have managed to land a bargain.

Visiting churches and monasteries

No one is admitted to churches and monasteries without being appropriately dressed, i.e. with knees and shoulders covered. Other things to remember if you don't wish to cause offence: don't clasp your hands behind your back, don't point at icons (be very careful about pointing in general) and never turn your back on the iconostasis in a church. When visiting monasteries and convents at midday, bear in mind that the monks and nuns usually take a short rest at that time.

Hospitality

If you're invited for a cup of coffee, remember that it's considered impolite to leave before the coffee cup has gone cold.

Cabarets

When looking for evening entertainment, be aware that a Cypriot cabaret is not much more than a glorified brothel.

Road Atlas of Cyprus

Please refer to back cover for an overview of this Road Atlas

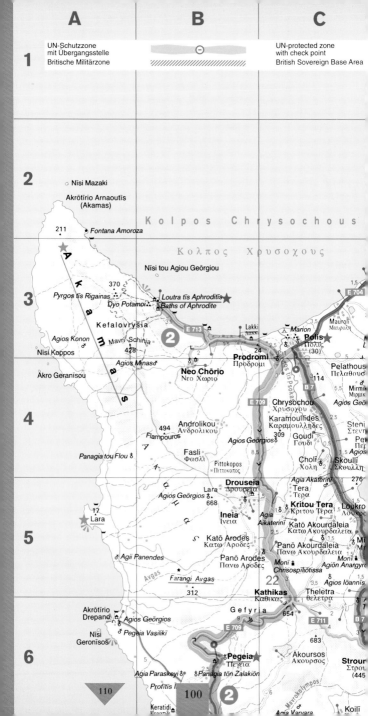

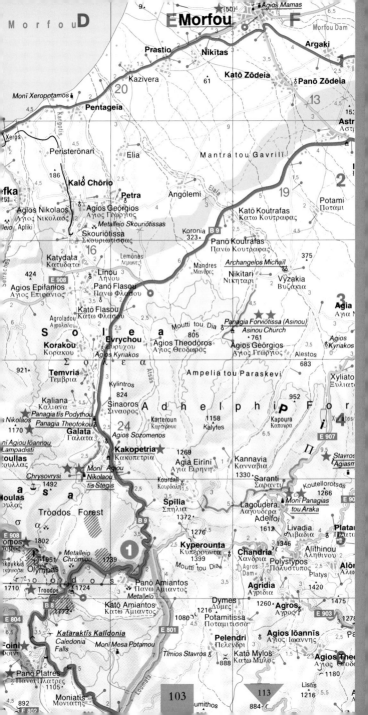

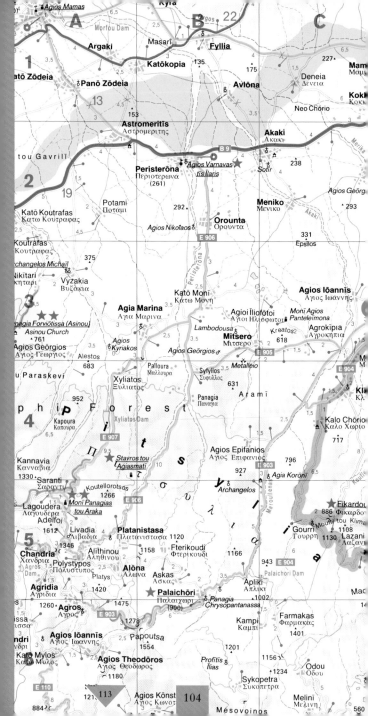

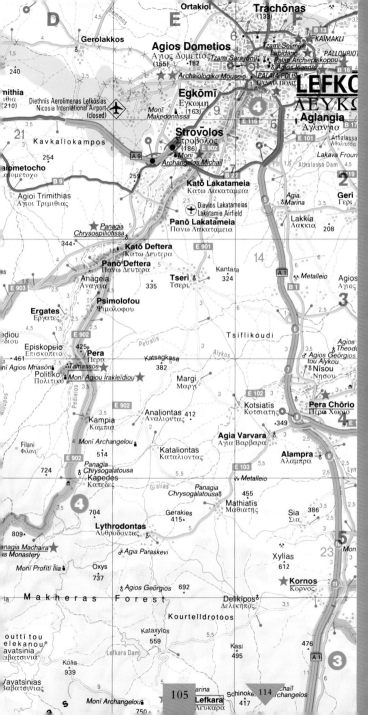

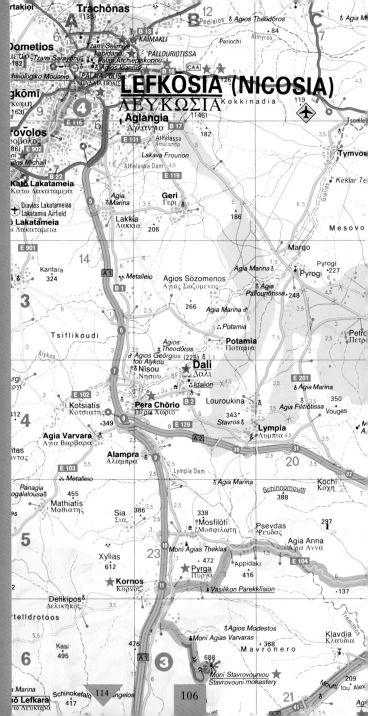

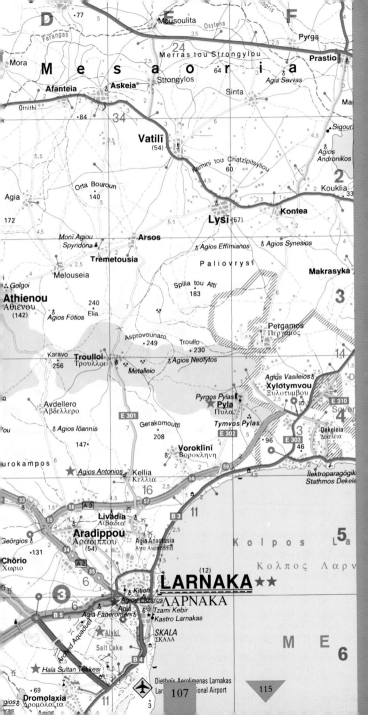

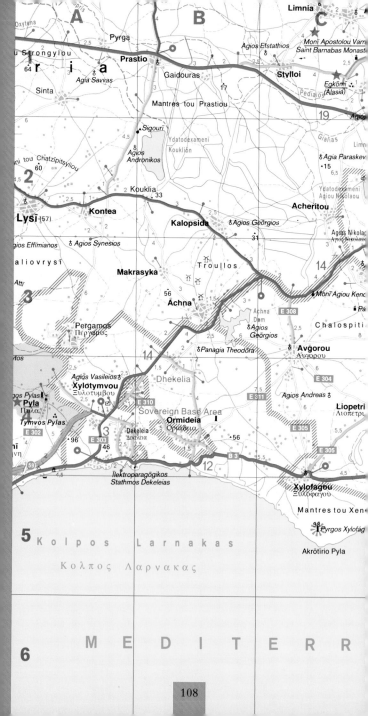

Limnia

A B C

Oxytona

Pyrga

u Strongylou Prastio

64

Agia Savvas

Sinta Gaidouras

Mantres tou Prastiou

Sigouri

Agios
Androni̇kos

ni tou Chatzipitsyliou

60

Kouklia 33

Lysi (57) Kontea

gios Effimianos Agios Synesios

aliovrysi

Atti

Pergamos
Πέργαμος

rtos

14

Agios Vasileios
Xylotymvou
Ξυλοτύμβου

os Pylas

Pyla Tymvos Pylas
Πύλα

E 302

ni̇
νη

Agios Efstathios

Moni Apostolou Varn
Saint Barnabas Monast

Styloi

Egkomi
(Alasia)

Pediaios

Agio

Gialias Lim

Agia Paraskev
•15

Ydatodexameni 6,5
Koukli̇on

Acheritou

Ydatodexameni
Agiou Nikolaou

Kalopsida Agios Geörgios

31

Agios Nikolar
Άγιος Νικόλαο

Troullos 14

Makrasyka

56 3

Achna 1,5

Achna
Dam

Agios
Geörgios

Moni Agiou Kenc

Pa

Chalospiti

Avgorou
Αυγόρου

E 304

Panagia Theodora

E 308

Dhekelia

E 310

Sovereign Base Area

Ormideia
Ορμίδεια

Dekeleia
Δεκέλεια

46

•96 E 303

59

Ilektroparagōgikos
Stathmos Dekeleias

2,5

3

7,5

Agios Andreas

E 311

12

E 305

Liopetri
Λιοπέτρι

5,5

E 305

Xylofagoú
Ξυλοφάγου

Mantres tou Xen

Pyrgos Xylofag

Akrótirio Pyla

5 Kolpos Larnakas
Κόλπος Λαρνακας

6 M E D I T E R R

108

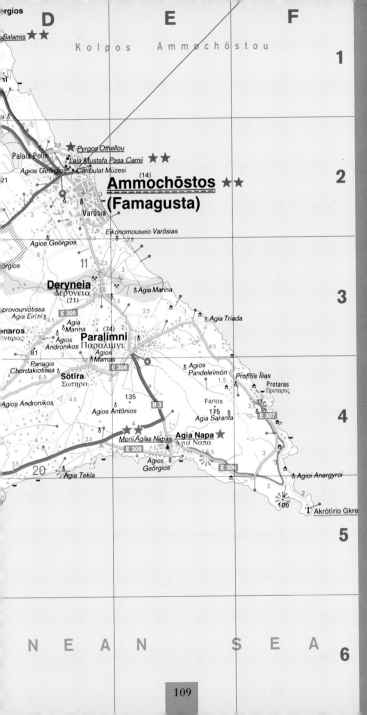

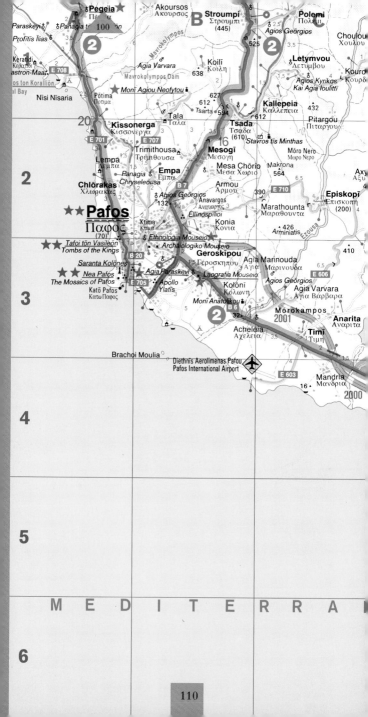

Pegeia ★
Πέγεια

Akoursos
Ακούρσος

B **Stroumpi**
Στρούμπι
(445)

Polemi
Πόλεμι

Paraskevi
Panagia te 100 on
Profitis Ilias

Agios Georgios

Choulou
Χούλου

2

525

Mavrokolympos

2

3.5

Letymvou
Λετύμβου

Kourd
Κουρδ

Kerati
astron-Maa
os ton Korallion
al Bay

E 708

Agia Varvara

Koili
Κοίλη
638

Agios Kyrikos
Kai Agia Ioulitti

Nisi Nisaria

Pótima
Πότιμα

Mavrokolympos Dam

Moni Agiou Neofytou

627
612
Tsarta
594

Kallepeia
Καλλέπεια

432

Pitargou
Πιταργου

20

Kissonerga
Κισσόνεργα

Tala
Τάλα

Tsada
Τσάδα
(610)

612

Stavros tis Minthas

E 701

E 707

16

Mesogi
Μεσόγι

Móro Nero
Μωρο Νερο

Lempa
Λέμπα

Trimithousa
Τριμηθούσα

Empa
Έμπα

Mesa Chório
Μέσα Χωριό

Makrona
564

Ax
Αξ

2

Chlórakas
Χλώρακας

Panagia
Chryseleousa

Agios Geórgios
132

Armou
Άρμού

390

E 710

Episkopi
Επισκοπή
(200)

Anavargos
Αναυαργος

Marathounta
Μαραθουντα

★★ **Pafos**
Πάφος
(701)

Ktima
Κτιμα

Ellinospilioi

Konia
Κόνια

426
Arminiatis

410

Ethnologia Mouseio

★★ Tafoi tōn Vasileōn
Tombs of the Kings

Archaiologiko Mouseio

Agia Marinouda
Αγια Μαρινουδα

6.5

Saranta Kolónes

B 20

Agia Paraskevi

Laografia Mouseio

Geroskipou
Γεροσκήπου

Agios Georgios

E 606

★★ Nea Pafós
The Mosaics of Pafos

E 705

Apollo
Ylatis

Kolóni
Κόλωνη

Agia Varvara
Αγια Βαρβαρα

Kató Pafos
Κατω Παφος

Moni Anatolikou

2
32

Mórokampos
2001

Anarita
Αναριτα

Acheleia
Αχελεια

3.5

Timi
Τιμη

Brachoi Moulia

Diethnīs Aerolimenas Pafou
Pafos International Airport

E 603

Mandria
Μάνδρια

16

2000

M E D I T E R R A

5

6

110

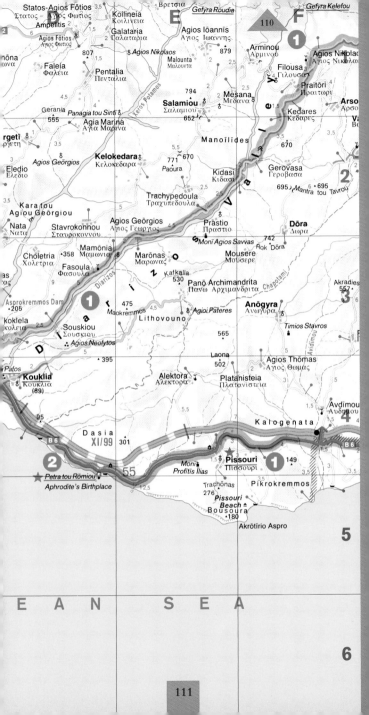

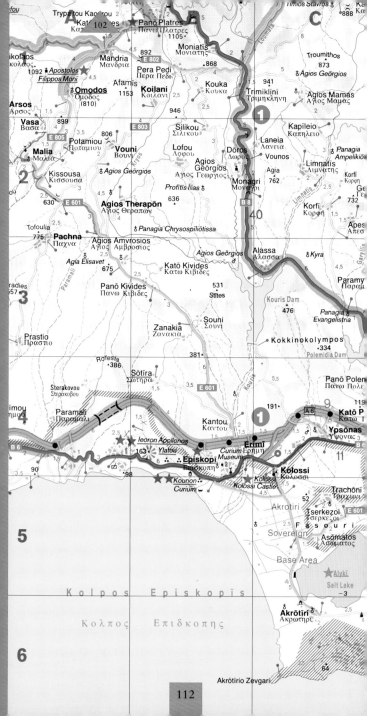

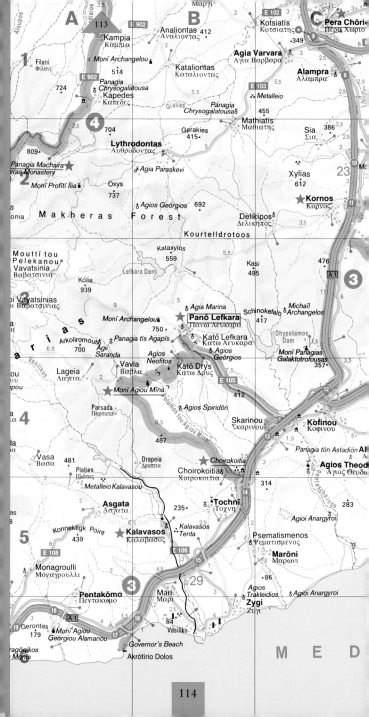

ROAD ATLAS LEGEND

German		English
Autobahn · Gebührenpflichtige Anschlußstelle · Gebührenstelle · Anschlußstelle mit Nummer · Rasthaus mit Übernachtung · Raststätte · Erfrischungsstelle · Tankstelle · Parkplatz mit und ohne WC	Trento	Motorway · Toll junction · Toll station · Junction with number · Motel · Restaurant · Snackbar · Filling-station · Parking place with and without WC
Autobahn in Bau und geplant mit Datum der Verkehrsübergabe	Datum ___ Date	Motorway under construction and projected with completion date
Zweibahnige Straße (4-spurig)		Dual carriageway (4 lanes)
Bundesstraße · Straßennummern	14 E45	Federal road · Road numbers
Wichtige Hauptstraße		Important main road
Hauptstraße · Tunnel · Brücke	)=(	Main road · Tunnel · Bridge
Nebenstraßen		Minor roads
Fahrweg · Fußweg		Track · Footpath
Wanderweg (Auswahl)		Tourist footpath (selection)
Eisenbahn mit Fernverkehr		Main line railway
Zahnradbahn, Standseilbahn		Rack-railway, funicular
Kabinenschwebebahn · Sessellift		Aerial cableway · Chair-lift
Autofähre	●	Car ferry
Personenfähre		Passenger ferry
Schiffahrtslinie		Shipping route
Naturschutzgebiet · Sperrgebiet		Nature reserve · Prohibited area
Nationalpark, Naturpark · Wald		National park, natural park · Forest
Straße für Kfz gesperrt	X X X X X	Road closed to motor vehicles
Straße mit Gebühr		Toll road
Straße mit Wintersperre	XII-II	Road closed in winter
Straße für Wohnanhänger gesperrt bzw. nicht empfehlenswert		Road closed or not recommended for caravans
Touristenstraße · Paß	Weinstraße ⌒1510	Tourist route · Pass
Schöner Ausblick · Rundblick · Landschaftlich bes. schöne Strecke		Scenic view · Panoramic view · Route with beautiful scenery
Golfplatz · Schwimmbad		Golf-course · Swimming pool
Ferienzeltplatz · Zeltplatz		Holiday camp · Transit camp
Jugendherberge · Sprungschanze		Youth hostel · Ski jump
Kirche im Ort, freistehend · Kapelle		Church · Chapel
Kloster · Klosterruine		Monastery · Monastery ruin
Schloß, Burg · Schloß-, Burgruine		Palace, castle · Ruin
Turm · Funk-, Fernsehturm		Tower · Radio-, TV-tower
Leuchtturm · Kraftwerk		Lighthouse · Power station
Wasserfall · Schleuse		Waterfall · Lock
Bauwerk · Marktplatz, Areal	▪	Important building · Market place, area
Ausgrabungs- u. Ruinenstätte · Feldkreuz	⁂	Arch. excavation, ruins · Calvary
Dolmen · Menhir	π	Dolmen · Menhir
Hünen-, Hügelgrab · Soldatenfriedhof	☆	Cairn · Military cemetery
Hotel, Gasthaus, Berghütte · Höhle		Hotel, inn, refuge · Cave

Kultur		**Culture**
Malerisches Ortsbild · Ortshöhe	**WIEN** (171)	Picturesque town · Elevation
Eine Reise wert	★★ **MILANO**	Worth a journey
Lohnt einen Umweg	★ TEMPLIN	Worth a detour
Sehenswert	Andermatt	Worth seeing
Landschaft Eine Reise wert	★★ **Las Cañadas**	**Landscape** Worth a journey
Lohnt einen Umweg	★ Texel	Worth a detour
Sehenswert	Dikti	Worth seeing

4 km
2 mi

INDEX

This index lists all the main places and sights mentioned in this guide. Page numbers in bold typeface indicate main entries; page numbers in italics refer to photos

What do you get for your money?

Rates of exchange differ from day to day — check the newspaper for current exchange rates. For the visitor it is important to know what to expect to pay for admission charges, eating and drinking. Here are a few prices to give you an idea of what your money is worth.

For CYP 6-8 per person you can have a substantial evening meal. A bottle of wine in a restaurant costs CYP 2-6. The same bottle of wine costs only 80-120c in a shop. A cup of Cypriot mocha costs 30-60c and a Nescafé 50-90c. The famous brandy sour will set you back 100-160c. A kilo of oranges bought at any market costs upwards of 30c and a kilo of potatoes only 25c, whereas a kilo of pork starts at CYP 1.30 at the butcher's.

Renting a deck-chair with an umbrella on the beach costs about CYP 1-2 a day. Surfboards start at CYP 4 an hour and surfing lessons for beginners cost CYP 6 an hour. A water-skiing session generally costs about CYP 7, but can run to more. Day trips are organized by travel agents for 9-12 CYP. A hire car starts at CYP 10 a day. The bus fare, if you take the regular buses the entire length of the south coast from Agía Nápa to Páfos, is only CYP 3.35. A litre of petrol is currently 38c.

CYP	£	US $	Can.$
1	1.15	1.86	2.81
2	2.30	3.71	5.62
3	3.45	5.57	8.43
4	4.60	7.43	11.24
5	5.75	9.28	14.05
6	6.90	11.14	16.86
7	8.05	13.00	19.67
8	9.20	14.85	22.48
9	10.35	16.71	25.29
10	11.50	18.56	28.10
15	17.25	27.85	42.14
20	22.10	37.13	56.19
25	28.74	46.41	70.24
30	34.50	55.70	84.28
40	46.00	74.26	112.38
50	57.49	92.83	140.47
75	86.23	139.24	210.71
100	115.00	185.65	280.94
250	287.44	464.13	702.36
500	574.88	928.25	1404.72
1000	1149.75	1856.50	2809.44